cook's library

Baking

cook's library

Baking

p

This is a Parragon Book
First published in 2003

Parragon
Queen Street House
4 Queen Street
Bath BA1 1HE, UK

ISBN: 0-75258-754-4

Printed in China

NOTE

This book uses metric and imperial measurements. Follow the same
units of measurement throughout; do not mix metric and imperial.
All spoon measurements are level: teaspoons are assumed to be 5 ml,
and tablespoons are assumed to be 15 ml. Unless otherwise stated,
milk is assumed to be full fat, eggs and individual vegetables such as
potatoes are medium, and pepper is freshly ground black pepper.

The times given for each recipe are an approximate guide only because the
preparation times may differ according to the techniques used by different
people and the cooking times may vary as a result of the type of oven used.
The preparation times include chilling and marinating times, where appropriate.

Recipes using raw or very lightly cooked eggs should be
avoided by infants, the elderly, pregnant women, convalescents,
and anyone suffering from an illness.

Contents

Introduction

It may be a daunting prospect to cook your own savoury bakes, tarts, bread and cakes instead of buying them at the supermarket, but once you have acquired the basic skills – and armed yourself with a few of the 'tricks' – it becomes fun, versatile and rewarding.

There are a few points that will ensure your baking session is successful, regardless of the type of recipe you have chosen. So, before you start:

- Read through the recipe carefully, and make sure you have the right ingredients – using plain flour when self-raising flour is specified, for example, may not produce the result you were expecting!

- Remember to preheat the oven to the required temperature.

- Make sure that you are using the correct size and shape of tin or dish, because the quantities given in the recipe are for the size of the tin specified.

- Prepare the cookware before you start assembling any of the ingredients – grease or line tins, dishes or baking sheets as directed in the recipe.

- Weigh all the ingredients accurately, and do any basic preparation, such as chopping, slicing or grating, before you start cooking.

- Once you start cooking, follow the recipe step-by-step, in the order given. Using high-quality ingredients will give the best results – unbleached flours and unrefined sugars are all readily available and are best for cakes, while fresh vegetables, fish and meat from a reliable supplier, and a good, extra virgin olive oil will make all the difference to your savoury bakes.

Pastry

- Metal tins, not porcelain dishes, are best for quiches and tarts.

- Use fat at room temperature, cut into small pieces.

- Use ice-cold water for mixing.

- Pastry benefits from cool ingredients and cold hands.

- Always sift the dry ingredients into a large mixing bowl, to incorporate air.

- Wrap the pastry in foil and leave it to 'rest' in the refrigerator for 30 minutes before using.

Bread

- Plan ahead – most bread recipes include one or two 'provings' (leaving the dough in a warm place to double its bulk).

- If the flour feels quite cool, warm it gently in an oven at a low temperature.

- Make sure the liquid is hand-hot, to activate the yeast.

- To knead dough, stretch it away from you with one hand while pulling it towards you with the other, then fold in the edges, give it a quarter turn, and repeat.

- To test whether bread is cooked, tap the base – it should sound hollow if it is done.

Cakes

- Using a loose-bottomed tin will make it much easier to turn out the cake.

- Bring all the ingredients to room temperature before assembling.

- If possible, use a hand-held electric mixer for 'creaming' (beating the butter and sugar together until the mixture has a 'soft dropping' consistency).

- 'Fold in' the dry ingredients very gently, using a metal spoon or spatula in a figure-of-eight movement. This lets the air get to the mixture and stops the cake becoming too heavy.

- When the cake is cooked, it should feel springy when pressed lightly. Alternatively, insert a clean fine metal skewer into the centre of the cake – if it is cooked, the skewer should come out clean.

Traditional Cooking

Trends in eating have changed enormously in recent years to fit in with a greater awareness of health and a busier lifestyle, becoming lighter, healthier and far more cosmopolitan. But one tradition has survived – the British afternoon tea – which many people still enjoy today. Although it is often restricted to rest days and holidays, the aroma of freshly baked scones, muffins, biscuits, teabreads and cakes is as enticing as ever.

Tea-time enthusiasts can progress through the year enjoying treats made with seasonal ingredients. Dark winter evenings may be cheered by a deliciously moist Banana and Date Loaf; home-made Teacakes, crammed with dried fruit and glazed with honey, served toasted, perhaps over a log fire; or a rich buttery Clementine Cake.

Later in the year, the arrival of summer is celebrated by a leisurely tea in the garden. Cherry Scones, still warm from the oven, might be followed by Strawberry Roulade, a light sponge with a fruity fromage frais filling, topped with toasted almonds and dusted with icing sugar.

The onset of the cooler autumn days is lightened by the year's harvest. A glut of apples can be turned into a Spiced Apple Ring, or Crispy-topped Fruit Bake – an easy-to-make cake decorated with apples and delicious served with cream – while the addition of roasted pumpkin flesh makes an unusual and flavoursome Pumpkin Loaf.

At any time of year, the tea table can be enhanced by a plate of crisp, melting Shortbread Fantails, or one of the many fruit cake recipes – surely a good reason to start baking.

Equally appetizing, but in a totally different way, are the baking aromas that float from the kitchen of an Italian cook. Here, pasta – in the form of lasagne, cannelloni or any of the wide variety of shapes – is often served mixed with a sauce of vegetables, fish or meat, topped with cheese and baked until golden. Spinach and Mushroom Lasagne, Pasticcio and Prawn Pasta Bake are just a few examples. Home-made bread is flavoured with olives, herbs, cheese, peppers or sun-dried tomatoes, and, of course, garlic is a favourite ingredient in many recipes.

From Italy, too, comes that universal favourite, pizza, said to have been created in Naples. A dough base, spread with a tomato sauce slowly reduced until thick, is topped with a mixture of vegetables and perhaps some Italian sausage, deliciously stringy mozzarella cheese, olives, anchovies, a sprinkling of herbs and a drizzle of olive oil – the possible combinations are endless, and the end results are wonderful. There are plenty of recipes to choose from, such as the classic Pizza Margherita or a delicious Onion, Ham and Cheese Pizza.

The basic recipe for risotto, a versatile Italian rice dish, can be combined with vegetables and cheese, bound with eggs and baked to make dishes such as Green Easter Pie.

To round off their meals, Italian cooks often make use of cream and soft, creamy cheeses in desserts, as in the fresh Mascarpone Cheesecake, which is studded with stem ginger, or the Tuscan Pudding, which is delicious served with cream or crème fraîche.

Basic Recipes

These recipes form the basis of several of the dishes contained in this book. Many of these basic recipes can be made in advance and stored in the refrigerator until required.

Savoury Pastry

MAKES 1 x 20-cm/8-inch flan base

175 g/6 oz plain flour, plus extra for dusting
pinch of salt
6 tbsp butter, plus extra for greasing
2–3 tbsp water

1 Mix the flour and salt together in a bowl. Rub in the butter, then add the water and mix to form a soft dough. Wrap in clingfilm and leave to chill for 30 minutes.

2 Grease a 20-cm/8-inch flan tin. Roll out the dough on a lightly floured work surface and use to line the tin. Prick the dough with a fork, then cover with clingfilm and leave to chill for 30 minutes.

3 Line the pastry base with foil and fill with baking beans. Bake in a preheated oven, 200°C/400°F/Gas Mark 6, for 10–12 minutes until golden. Remove from the oven, discard the baking beans and foil, then bake for a further 10 minutes.

4 Remove from the oven, then add your chosen filling and cook as in main recipe.

Sweet Pastry

MAKES 1 x 24-cm/9½-inch flan base

150 g/5½ oz plain flour, plus extra for dusting
25 g/1 oz caster sugar
125 g/4½ oz butter, plus extra for greasing
1 tbsp water

1 Mix the flour and sugar together in a bowl, then rub in the butter. Add the water and mix to form a soft dough. Wrap in clingfilm and leave to chill for 30 minutes

2 Grease a 24-cm/9½-inch flan tin. Roll out the dough on a lightly floured work surface and use to line the tin. Prick the dough with a fork, then cover with clingfilm and chill in the refrigerator for 30 minutes.

3 Line the pastry base with foil and fill with baking beans. Bake in a preheated oven, 190°C/375°F/Gas Mark 5, for 15 minutes. Remove from the oven, discard the baking beans and foil, then bake for 15 minutes.

4 Remove from the oven, then add your chosen filling and cook as in main recipe.

Basic Pasta Dough

MAKES about 250 g/9 oz pasta

125 g/4½ oz strong plain flour, plus extra for dusting
125 g/4½ oz fine semolina
1 tsp salt
1 tbsp olive oil
2 eggs
1–2 tbsp hot water

1 Sift together the flour, semolina and salt in a bowl and make a well in the centre. Pour in the olive oil and add the eggs. Add 1 tablespoon of hot water and, using your fingertips, work to form a smooth dough. Sprinkle on a little more water if necessary to make the dough pliable.

2 Knead the dough on a lightly floured work surface for about 10–15 minutes until smooth and elastic. Dust the dough with more flour if your fingers become sticky.

3 Divide the dough into 2 equal pieces. Cover a work surface with a tea towel and dust it liberally with flour. Place 1 portion of the dough on the floured tea towel and roll it out as thinly and evenly as possible,

stretching the dough gently until the pattern of the weave shows through. Cover it with a separate tea towel. Roll out the second piece in the same way.

4 Use a ruler and a sharp knife to cut long, thin strips for noodles, or small confectionery cutters to cut rounds, star shapes or even an assortment of other shapes. Cover the dough shapes with a clean tea towel and leave in a cool place (not a refrigerator) for 30–45 minutes to become partly dry. To dry ribbons, place a tea towel over the back of a chair and hang the ribbons over it. Use this fresh pasta in the recipe of your choice.

Basic Pizza Dough

MAKES 1 x 25-cm/10-inch pizza

175 g/6 oz plain flour, plus extra for dusting
1 tsp salt
1 tsp easy-blend dried yeast
6 tbsp hand-hot water
1 tbsp olive oil

1 Sift the flour and salt into a large bowl and add the yeast. Pour in the water and olive oil and mix to a dough. Knead for 5 minutes, then leave to 'prove' until doubled in size.

2 Knock out the air from the dough, then knead lightly. Roll out on a floured work surface, ready for use.

Ragù Sauce

MAKES about 600 ml/1 pint

3 tbsp olive oil
40 g/1½ oz butter
2 large onions, chopped
4 celery sticks, sliced thinly
175 g/6 oz streaky bacon, chopped
2 garlic cloves, chopped
500 g/1 lb 2 oz beef mince
2 tbsp tomato purée
1 tbsp plain flour
400 g/14 oz canned chopped tomatoes
150 ml/5 fl oz beef stock
150 ml/5 fl oz red wine
2 tsp dried oregano
½ tsp freshly grated nutmeg
salt and pepper

1 Heat the oil and butter in a large pan over a medium heat. Add the onions, celery and bacon and fry for 5 minutes, stirring constantly.

2 Stir in the garlic and beef mince and cook, stirring constantly, until the meat is completely sealed. Reduce the heat and simmer for 10 minutes, stirring occasionally.

3 Increase the heat to medium, stir in the tomato purée and flour and cook for 1–2 minutes. Add the chopped tomatoes, stock and wine and bring to the boil, stirring constantly. Season to taste with salt and pepper, then stir in the oregano and nutmeg. Reduce the heat, then cover and simmer for 45 minutes. The sauce is now ready to use.

Italian Cheese Sauce

MAKES about 300 ml/10 fl oz

2 tbsp butter
25 g/1 oz plain flour
300 ml/10 fl oz hot milk
pinch of freshly grated nutmeg
pinch of dried thyme
2 tbsp white wine vinegar
3 tbsp double cream
55 g/2 oz freshly grated mozzarella cheese
55 g/2 oz freshly grated Parmesan cheese
1 tsp English mustard
2 tbsp soured cream
salt and pepper

1 Melt the butter in a pan and stir in the flour. Cook, stirring, until the roux is light and crumbly. Gradually stir in the milk. Cook, stirring, for 10 minutes until thick and smooth.

2 Add the nutmeg, thyme, vinegar and seasoning. Stir in the double cream, add the cheeses, mustard and soured cream and mix until blended.

Pesto Sauce

MAKES about 300 ml/10 fl oz

55 g/2 oz fresh parsley, chopped finely
2 garlic cloves, crushed
55 g/2 oz pine kernels, crushed
2 tbsp chopped fresh basil leaves
55 g/2 oz freshly grated Parmesan cheese
150 ml/5 fl oz olive oil
white pepper

1 Put all the ingredients into a blender or food processor and process for 2 minutes. Season with white pepper, transfer to a jug, cover and chill until ready to use.

How to Use This Book

Each recipe contains a wealth of useful information, including a breakdown of nutritional quantities, preparation and cooking times, and level of difficulty. All of this information is explained in detail below.

A full-colour photograph of the finished dish.

The ingredients for each recipe are listed in the order that they are used.

The nutritional information provided for each recipe is per serving or per portion. Optional ingredients, variations or serving suggestions have not been included in the calculations.

The method is clearly explained with step-by-step instructions that are easy to follow.

Cook's Tips provide useful information regarding ingredients or cooking techniques.

17

BAKING

This simple combination of fudgey meringue topped with fromage frais and raspberries is the perfect finale to any meal.

Brown Sugar Pavlovas

SERVES 4
2 large egg whites
1 tsp cornflour
1 tsp raspberry vinegar
100 g/3½ oz light muscovado sugar, crushed free of lumps
2 tbsp redcurrant jelly
2 tbsp unsweetened orange juice
150 ml/5 fl oz low-fat fromage frais
175 g/6 oz raspberries, thawed if frozen
rose-scented geranium leaves, to decorate (optional)

1 Line a large baking tray with baking paper. Whisk the egg whites until very stiff and dry. Gently fold in the cornflour and vinegar.

2 Gradually whisk in the sugar, a spoonful at a time, until the mixture is thick and glossy.

3 Divide the mixture into 4 and spoon on to the baking tray, spaced well apart. Smooth each portion into a round, about 10 cm/4 inches across and bake in a preheated oven, 150°C/300°C/Gas Mark 2, for 40–45 minutes until lightly browned and crisp. Remove from the oven and leave to cool on the baking tray.

4 Place the redcurrant jelly and orange juice in a small pan and heat, stirring, until melted. Leave to cool for 10 minutes.

5 Using a palette knife, carefully remove each pavlova from the baking paper and transfer to a serving plate. Top with the fromage frais and the raspberries. Brush the fruit with the redcurrant and orange glaze, and decorate with the geranium leaves, if using.

NUTRITION
Calories 155; Sugars 34 g; Protein 5 g; Carbohydrate 35 g; Fat 0.2 g; Saturates 0 g

COOK'S TIP
Make a large pavlova by forming the meringue into a single round, measuring 18 cm/7 inches across, on a lined baking tray and bake for 1 hour.

easy
1 hr
1 hr

The number of stars represents the difficulty of each recipe, ranging from very easy (1 star) to challenging (4 stars).

This amount of time represents the preparation of ingredients, including cooling, chilling and soaking times.

This represents the cooking time.

Snacks *and* Starters

With so many fresh ingredients readily available, it is very easy to create some deliciously different starters to make the perfect introduction to any meal. The ideas in this chapter are an inspiration to cook and a treat to eat, and they give an edge to the appetite that makes the main course even more enjoyable. When choosing a starter, make sure that you provide a good balance of flavours, colours and textures that offer plenty of variety and contrast. Balance the nature of the recipes too – a rich main course is best preceded by a light starter to stimulate the taste buds.

This dish combines layers of aubergine, tomato sauce, mozzarella and Parmesan cheese to create a very tasty starter.

Aubergine Bake

SERVES 4

3–4 tbsp olive oil
2 garlic cloves, crushed
2 large aubergines
100 g/3½ oz mozzarella cheese, sliced thinly
200 ml/7 fl oz passata
50 g/1¾ oz freshly grated Parmesan cheese
assorted salad leaves, to serve

1 Heat 2 tablespoons of the olive oil in a large, heavy-based frying pan over a low heat. Add the garlic and sauté for 30 seconds.

2 Slice the aubergines lengthways. Add the slices to the frying pan and cook for 3–4 minutes on each side or until tender. (You will probably have to cook them in batches, so add the remaining oil as necessary.)

3 Remove the aubergines with a slotted spoon and drain on kitchen paper.

4 Place a layer of aubergine slices in a large, shallow ovenproof dish and cover with a layer of mozzarella cheese, then pour over one-third of the passata. Continue layering in the same order, finishing with a layer of passata on top.

5 Sprinkle the Parmesan cheese evenly over the top and bake in a preheated oven, 200°C/400°F/Gas Mark 6, for about 25–30 minutes or until the top is golden and bubbling.

6 Transfer the bake to 4 large serving plates and serve warm or chilled with salad leaves.

NUTRITION

Calories *232*; Sugars *8 g*; Protein *10 g*;
Carbohydrate *8 g*; Fat *18 g*; Saturates *6 g*

 moderate

5 mins

45 mins

This is an impressive dinner-party dish served as a starter. You will find large tomatoes are easier to fill.

Stuffed Tomatoes

1 Rinse the tomatoes, cut off the tops and scoop out the flesh. Grease an ovenproof dish with the butter and place the tomatoes in the dish.

2 Heat the vegetable oil in a large, heavy-based saucepan over a medium heat. Add the onion and fry until golden.

3 Reduce the heat and add the ginger, garlic, pepper, salt and garam masala. Stir-fry the mixture for 3–5 minutes.

4 Add the lamb mince to the pan and fry for about 10–15 minutes or until it has lost its pink colour.

5 Add the chilli and coriander leaves and continue stir-frying the mixture for 3–5 minutes.

6 Spoon the lamb mixture into the tomatoes and replace the tops. Cook the tomatoes in a preheated oven, 180°C/350°F/Gas Mark 4, for 15–20 minutes.

7 Transfer the tomatoes to 4 serving plates, garnish with lemon wedges and serve hot with salad leaves.

 COOK'S TIP

You could use the same recipe to fill red or green peppers, if you prefer.

SERVES 4

6 large, firm tomatoes
4 tbsp unsalted butter
5 tbsp vegetable oil
1 onion, chopped finely
1 tsp fresh root ginger, chopped finely
1 tsp crushed fresh garlic
1 tsp pepper
1 tsp salt
½ tsp garam masala
450 g/1 lb lamb mince
1 fresh green chilli, deseeded and finely chopped
handful of fresh coriander leaves
lemon wedges, to garnish
salad leaves, to serve

NUTRITION
Calories 290; Sugars 5 g; Protein 17 g; Carbohydrate 8 g; Fat 23 g; Saturates 9 g

⭐⭐⭐ moderate

🟢 5 mins

🔵 45 mins

Ready-made pizza bases are covered with a chilli-flavoured tomato sauce and topped with kidney beans, cheese and green jalapeño chillies.

Mexican-style Pizzas

SERVES 4

4 ready-made individual pizza bases
1 tbsp olive oil
200 g/7 oz canned chopped tomatoes with garlic and herbs
2 tbsp tomato purée
200 g/7 oz canned kidney beans, drained and rinsed
115 g/4 oz sweetcorn kernels, thawed if frozen
1–2 tsp chilli sauce
1 large red onion, shredded
100 g/3½ oz reduced-fat mature Cheddar cheese, grated
1 large fresh green jalapeño chilli, deseeded and sliced into rings
salt and pepper

1 Arrange the pizza bases on a baking tray and brush them with the olive oil.

2 Mix the tomatoes, tomato purée, kidney beans and sweetcorn together in a bowl and add chilli sauce to taste. Season with salt and pepper.

3 Using a spoon, spread the tomato and kidney bean mixture evenly over each pizza base to cover.

4 Top each pizza with shredded onion and sprinkle with some grated Cheddar cheese and a few slices of green chilli to taste.

5 Bake in a preheated oven, 220°C/425°F/Gas Mark 7, for about 20 minutes or until the vegetables are tender, the cheese has melted and the base is crisp and golden.

6 Remove the pizzas from the baking tray and transfer to 4 warmed serving plates. Serve immediately.

NUTRITION
Calories 350; Sugars 8 g; Protein 18 g;
Carbohydrate 49 g; Fat 10 g; Saturates 3 g

easy

10 mins

20 mins

 COOK'S TIP

Serve a Mexican-style salad with this pizza. Arrange sliced tomatoes, fresh coriander leaves and a few slices of a small, ripe avocado on a platter. Sprinkle with fresh lime juice and coarse sea salt.

These crisp pies are filled with a tasty onion, garlic and parsley mixture, making them ideal for lunch boxes.

Cheese *and* Onion Pies

1 Heat the vegetable oil in a frying pan over a low heat. Add the onions and garlic and fry for 10–15 minutes or until the onions are softened. Remove the pan from the heat and stir in the parsley and cheese and season to taste with salt and pepper.

2 To make the pastry, sift the flour and salt into a large bowl. Add the butter and rub it in with your fingertips until the mixture resembles breadcrumbs. Gradually stir in the water and mix to form a dough.

3 Roll out the dough on a lightly floured work surface and divide it into 8 portions. Roll out each portion to a 10-cm/4-inch round and use half of the rounds to line 4 individual tart tins.

4 Fill each round with one-quarter of the cheese and onion mixture. Cover with the remaining 4 pastry rounds. Make a slit in the top of each tart with the point of a knife to allow steam to escape during cooking and seal the edges of the pies with the back of a teaspoon.

5 Bake in a preheated oven, 220°C/425°F/Gas Mark 7, for 20 minutes. Transfer the pies to 4 serving plates if serving hot or to a wire rack if serving cold.

COOK'S TIP

You can prepare the onion filling in advance and store it in the refrigerator until required.

SERVES 4

3 tbsp vegetable oil
4 onions, sliced thinly
4 garlic cloves, crushed
4 tbsp finely chopped fresh parsley
75 g/2¾ oz mature Cheddar cheese, grated
salt and pepper

pastry
175 g/6 oz plain flour, plus extra for dusting
½ tsp salt
100 g/3½ oz butter, cut into small pieces
3–4 tbsp water

NUTRITION
Calories *544*; Sugars *9 g*; Protein *11 g*; Carbohydrate *47 g*; Fat *36 g*; Saturates *18 g*

 easy

 15 mins

 35 mins

A crisp lining of bread is filled with garlic butter and pine kernels to make a delightful and unusual starter or snack.

Garlic *and* Pine Kernel Tarts

SERVES 4

4 slices wholemeal or Granary bread
50 g/1¾ oz pine kernels
150 g/5½ oz butter
5 garlic cloves, halved
2 tbsp chopped fresh oregano
4 stoned black olives, halved
fresh oregano sprigs, to garnish

1 Using a rolling pin, flatten the bread slightly. Using a pastry cutter, cut out 4 circles of bread to fit your individual tart tins – they should measure about 10 cm/4 inches across. Reserve the offcuts of bread and leave them in the refrigerator for 10 minutes or until required.

2 Meanwhile, place the pine kernels on a small baking tray and toast under a preheated hot grill for 2–3 minutes or until golden.

3 Put the reserved bread offcuts, pine kernels, butter, garlic and oregano into a food processor and process for about 20 seconds. Alternatively, pound the ingredients by hand with a mortar and pestle. The mixture should have a rough texture.

4 Spoon the pine kernel butter mixture into the lined tins and top with the olives. Bake in a preheated oven, 200°C/400°F/Gas Mark 6, for 10–15 minutes or until golden.

5 Transfer the tarts to 4 warmed serving plates, garnish with a few sprigs of fresh oregano and serve warm.

NUTRITION
Calories *435*; Sugars *1 g*; Protein *6 g*;
Carbohydrate *17 g*; Fat *39 g*; Saturates *20 g*

moderate

20 mins

20 mins

🍲 **COOK'S TIP**

Chill 200 g/7 oz puff pastry for 20 minutes, then use to line the tins. Cover with foil and bake blind for 10 minutes. Remove the foil and bake for 3–4 minutes. Cool. Continue from Step 2, adding 2 tablespoons of breadcrumbs to the mix.

This is an unusual Indian dish, in that the aubergines are first baked in the oven, then cooked in a saucepan.

Aubergines *and* Yogurt

1 Rinse the aubergines and pat dry with kitchen paper.

2 Place the aubergines in an ovenproof dish and bake in a preheated oven, 160°C/425°F/Gas Mark 3, for 45 minutes. Remove the aubergines from the oven and leave to cool.

3 Using a spoon, scoop out the aubergine flesh and reserve.

4 Heat the vegetable oil in a heavy-based saucepan over a medium heat. Add the onion and cumin seeds and fry, stirring constantly, for 1–2 minutes.

5 Add the chilli powder, salt, yogurt and mint sauce to the saucepan and stir well to mix. Reduce the heat.

6 Add the aubergine flesh to the onion and yogurt mixture and fry over a low heat, stirring constantly, for 5–7 minutes or until all of the liquid has been completely absorbed and the mixture is quite dry.

7 Transfer the aubergine and yogurt mixture to a warmed serving dish and garnish with shredded mint. Serve immediately with freshly cooked rice.

COOK'S TIP

Rich in protein and calcium, yogurt plays a very important part in Indian cooking. Thick natural yogurt most closely resembles the yogurt made in many Indian homes.

SERVES 4

2 medium aubergines
4 tbsp vegetable oil
1 onion, sliced
1 tsp white cumin seeds
1 tsp chilli powder
1 tsp salt
3 tbsp natural yogurt
½ tsp mint sauce
shredded fresh mint, to garnish
freshly cooked brown rice, to serve

NUTRITION
Calories *147*; Sugars *6 g*; Protein *3 g*;
Carbohydrate *8 g*; Fat *11 g*; Saturates *1 g*

easy

5 mins

1 hr 5 mins

This is a classic combination in which the smooth, creamy cheese balances the sharper taste of the spinach.

Spinach *and* Ricotta Shells

SERVES 4

400 g/14 oz dried lumache rigate grande pasta
5 tbsp olive oil
55 g/2 oz fresh white breadcrumbs
125 ml/4 fl oz milk
300 g/10½ oz frozen spinach, thawed and drained
225 g/8 oz ricotta cheese
pinch of freshly grated nutmeg
400 g/14 oz canned chopped tomatoes, drained
1 garlic clove, crushed
salt and pepper

1 Bring a large saucepan of lightly salted water to the boil over a medium heat. Add the lumache and 1 tablespoon of the olive oil, bring back to the boil and cook for 8–10 minutes or until just tender, but still firm to the bite. Drain the pasta, refresh under cold running water, drain again and reserve until required.

2 Put the breadcrumbs, milk and 3 tablespoons of the remaining olive oil in a food processor and process to combine.

3 Add the spinach and ricotta cheese to the food processor and process to a smooth mixture. Transfer to a bowl, stir in the nutmeg and season to taste with salt and pepper.

4 Mix the tomatoes, garlic and the remaining olive oil together, then spoon the mixture into the base of a large ovenproof dish.

5 Using a teaspoon, fill the lumache with the spinach and ricotta mixture and arrange them on top of the tomato mixture in the dish. Cover with foil and bake in a preheated oven, 180°C/350°F/Gas Mark 4, for 20 minutes. Serve hot straight from the dish.

NUTRITION

Calories *672*; Sugars *10 g*; Protein *23 g*;
Carbohydrate *93 g*; Fat *26 g*; Saturates *8 g*

moderate

10 mins

40 mins

COOK'S TIP

Ricotta is a creamy Italian cheese traditionally made from ewes' milk whey. It is soft and white, with a smooth texture and a slightly sweet flavour. It should be used within 2–3 days of purchase.

This is a traditional Italian recipe but, for a less rich version, simply omit the eggs.

Gnocchi Romana

1 Pour the milk into a large saucepan and bring to the boil over a low heat. Remove the pan from the heat and stir in the nutmeg and 2 tablespoons of the butter. Season to taste with salt and pepper.

2 Gradually stir the semolina into the milk, whisking to prevent lumps from forming, and return the pan to a low heat. Simmer, stirring constantly, for about 10 minutes or until very thick.

3 Beat 55 g/2 oz of the Parmesan cheese into the semolina mixture, then beat in the eggs. Continue beating until smooth, then cool for a few minutes.

4 Spread out the cooled semolina mixture in a layer on a sheet of baking paper. Smooth the surface with a damp spatula – it should be 1 cm/½ inch thick. Leave to cool completely, then chill in the refrigerator for 1 hour.

5 Once chilled, cut out rounds of gnocchi, measuring about 4 cm/1½ inches in diameter, using a plain, greased pastry cutter.

6 Grease a shallow ovenproof dish or 4 individual ovenproof dishes. Arrange the gnocchi trimmings over the base of the dish or dishes, then cover them with the rounds of gnocchi, overlapping them slightly.

7 Melt the remaining butter and drizzle it over the gnocchi. Sprinkle over the remaining Parmesan cheese, then sprinkle the Gruyère cheese over the top.

8 Bake in a preheated oven, 200°C/400°F/Gas Mark 6, for 25–30 minutes or until crisp and golden-brown. Garnish with basil and serve with salad leaves.

SERVES 4

700 ml/1¼ pints milk
pinch of freshly grated nutmeg
6 tbsp butter, plus extra for greasing
225 g/8 oz semolina
125 g/4½ oz freshly grated Parmesan cheese
2 eggs, beaten
55 g/2 oz Gruyère cheese, grated
salt and pepper
fresh basil sprigs, to garnish
salad leaves, to serve

NUTRITION
Calories 709; Sugars 9 g; Protein 32 g;
Carbohydrate 58 g; Fat 41 g; Saturates 25 g

moderate

1 hr 15 mins

45 mins

Serve this dish while the cheese is still hot and melted, as cooked cheese turns very rubbery if it is allowed to cool down.

Three Cheese Bake

SERVES 4

1 tbsp butter, for greasing
400 g/14 oz dried penne
1 tbsp olive oil
2 eggs, beaten
350 g/12 oz ricotta cheese
4 fresh basil sprigs
100 g/3½ oz mozzarella or halloumi cheese, grated
70 g/2½ oz freshly grated Parmesan cheese
salt and pepper
fresh basil leaves, to garnish (optional)

1 Lightly grease a large ovenproof dish with the butter.

2 Bring a large saucepan of lightly salted water to the boil over a medium heat. Add the penne and olive oil, bring back to the boil and cook for about 8–10 minutes or until just tender but still firm to the bite. Drain the pasta and keep warm.

3 Beat the eggs into the ricotta cheese. Season to taste with salt and pepper.

4 Spoon half of the penne into the base of the prepared dish and cover with half of the basil leaves.

5 Spoon over half of the ricotta cheese mixture. Sprinkle over the mozzarella or halloumi cheese and top with the remaining basil leaves. Cover with the remaining penne, then spoon over the remaining ricotta cheese mixture. Lightly sprinkle the Parmesan cheese over the top.

6 Bake in a preheated oven, 190°C/375°F/Gas Mark 5, for 30–40 minutes or until golden-brown and the topping is hot and bubbling. Garnish with fresh basil leaves, if liked and serve immediately.

NUTRITION

Calories 710; Sugars 6 g; Protein 34 g; Carbohydrate 80 g; Fat 30 g; Saturates 16 g

★★★   moderate

      5 mins

🕐   1 hr

👨‍🍳 **COOK'S TIP**

Try substituting smoked Bavarian cheese for the mozzarella or halloumi and grated Cheddar cheese for the Parmesan cheese, for a slightly different, but just as delicious flavour.

These large pasta nests look impressive and taste delicious when presented filled with grilled mixed vegetables.

Vegetable Pasta Nests

1 Bring a large saucepan of lightly salted water to the boil over a medium heat. Add the spaghetti, bring back to the boil and cook for 8–10 minutes or until just tender but still firm to the bite. Drain and reserve.

2 Place the aubergine, courgette and pepper on a large baking tray.

3 Mix the olive oil and garlic together in a bowl and pour over the vegetables, tossing to coat all over.

4 Cook the vegetables under a preheated hot grill for 10 minutes, turning occasionally, until tender and lightly charred. Reserve and keep warm.

5 Lightly grease 4 Yorkshire pudding tins with a little butter and divide the spaghetti between them. Using 2 forks, curl the spaghetti to form nests.

6 Brush the pasta nests with the melted butter or margarine and sprinkle with the breadcrumbs. Bake in a preheated oven, 200°C/400°F/Gas Mark 6, for 15 minutes or until lightly golden. Remove the pasta nests from the tins and transfer to 4 serving plates. Divide the grilled vegetables between the pasta nests, season to taste with salt and pepper and garnish with a few sprigs of parsley. Serve hot.

COOK'S TIP

The Italian term *al dente* means 'to the bite' and describes cooked pasta that is not too soft, but still has a 'bite' to it.

SERVES 4

175 g/6 oz dried spaghetti
1 aubergine, halved and sliced
1 courgette, diced
1 red pepper, deseeded and diagonally chopped
6 tbsp olive oil
2 garlic cloves, crushed
4 tbsp butter or margarine, melted, plus extra for greasing
15 g/½ oz dry white breadcrumbs
salt and pepper
fresh flat-leaf parsley sprigs, to garnish

NUTRITION
Calories *392*; Sugars *1 g*; Protein *6 g*; Carbohydrate *32 g*; Fat *28 g*; Saturates *9 g*

   moderate

   25 mins

   40 mins

This warming and satisfying dish would make a tasty snack or even a light family supper on a dreary winter's day.

Macaroni Bake

SERVES 4

450 g/1 lb dried short-cut macaroni
1 tbsp olive oil
4 tbsp beef dripping or olive oil
450 g/1 lb potatoes, peeled and thinly sliced
450 g/1 lb onions, sliced
225 g/8 oz mozzarella cheese, grated
150 ml/5 fl oz double cream
salt and pepper
cracked black pepper, to garnish
crusty brown bread and butter, to serve

1 Bring a large saucepan of lightly salted water to the boil over a medium heat. Add the macaroni and olive oil, bring back to the boil and cook for 12 minutes or until just tender, but still firm to the bite. Drain thoroughly and reserve.

2 Melt the beef dripping or heat the oil in a large flameproof casserole over a low heat, then remove the casserole from the heat.

3 Make alternate layers of potatoes, onions, macaroni and grated mozzarella cheese in the casserole, seasoning well with salt and pepper between each layer and finishing with a layer of cheese on top. Finally, pour the cream over the top layer of cheese.

4 Bake in a preheated oven, 200°C/400°F/Gas Mark 6, for 25 minutes. Remove the casserole from the oven and carefully brown the top of the bake under a preheated hot grill.

5 Garnish the bake with cracked pepper and serve straight from the casserole with crusty brown bread and butter as a main course. Alternatively, serve as a vegetable accompaniment with your favourite main course.

NUTRITION
Calories 728; Sugars 11 g; Protein 17 g;
Carbohydrate 75 g; Fat 42 g; Saturates 23 g

★★★   moderate

🕐 15 mins

🕐 45 mins

👨‍🍳 **COOK'S TIP**

For a stronger flavour, use mozzarella affumicata, a smoked version of this cheese, or Gruyère cheese, instead of the mozzarella cheese.

This makes an excellent light dish when served with a topping of pesto or anchovy sauce and a crisp, green salad.

Pancetta *and* Pecorino Cakes

1 Grease a baking tray with butter. Grill the pancetta under a preheated hot grill until cooked. Leave the pancetta to cool, then chop finely.

2 Sift together the flour and a pinch of salt into a large bowl. Add the butter and rub it in with your fingertips until the mixture resembles breadcrumbs. Add the pancetta and one-third of the grated cheese.

3 Mix the milk, tomato ketchup and Worcestershire sauce together and add to the dry ingredients, mixing to form a soft dough.

4 Roll out the dough on a lightly floured board to make an 18-cm/7-inch round. Brush with a little milk to glaze and cut into 8 wedges.

5 Arrange the dough wedges on the prepared baking tray and sprinkle over the remaining grated cheese. Bake in a preheated oven, 200°C/400°F/Gas Mark 6, for 20 minutes.

6 Meanwhile, bring a large saucepan of lightly salted water to the boil over a medium heat. Add the farfalle and olive oil, bring back to the boil and cook for 8–10 minutes or until just tender but still firm to the bite. Drain and transfer to a large serving dish. Top with the pancetta and pecorino cakes. Serve with the sauce of your choice and a green salad.

SERVES 4

2 tbsp butter, plus extra for greasing
100 g/3½ oz pancetta, rind removed
225 g/8 oz self-raising flour, plus extra for dusting
75 g/2¾ oz pecorino cheese, grated
150 ml/5 fl oz milk, plus extra for glazing
1 tbsp tomato ketchup
1 tsp Worcestershire sauce
400 g/14 oz dried farfalle
1 tbsp olive oil
salt

to serve
3 tbsp Pesto Sauce (see page 15) or anchovy sauce (optional)
green salad

NUTRITION
Calories 619; Sugars 4 g; Protein 22 g; Carbohydrate 71 g; Fat 29 g; Saturates 8 g

✪✪✪✪ challenging

  20 mins

🕐 40 mins

These tomato-flavoured tarts should be eaten as fresh as possible to enjoy the flaky and crisp buttery puff pastry.

Fresh Tomato Tarts

SERVES 6

250 g/9 oz fresh ready-made puff pastry
1 egg, beaten
2 tbsp Pesto Sauce (see page 15)
6 plum tomatoes, sliced
salt and pepper
fresh thyme leaves, to garnish (optional)

1 Roll out the puff pastry on a lightly floured work surface, to a rectangle measuring 30 x 25 cm/12 x 10 inches.

2 Cut the rectangle in half and divide each half into 3 pieces to make 6 even-sized rectangles. Leave to chill in the refrigerator for 20 minutes.

3 Lightly score the edges of the pastry rectangles and brush them with the beaten egg.

4 Spread the pesto over the rectangles, dividing it equally between them, leaving a 2.5-cm/1-inch border around each one.

5 Arrange the tomato slices along the centre of each rectangle on top of the pesto. Season well with salt and pepper and lightly sprinkle with fresh thyme leaves, if using.

6 Bake in a preheated oven, 200°C/400°F/Gas Mark 6, for 15–20 minutes or until well risen and golden-brown.

7 Transfer the tomato tarts to 6 warmed serving plates and serve while they are still piping hot.

NUTRITION

Calories 217; Sugars 3 g; Protein 5 g;
Carbohydrate 18 g; Fat 14 g; Saturates 1 g

 moderate

 35 mins

 20 mins

🍴 COOK'S TIP

Instead of individual tarts, roll the pastry out to form 1 large rectangle. Spoon over the pesto and arrange the tomatoes over the top.

This tart is full of the colour and flavour of the courgettes and red and green peppers. It makes a great change from a Quiche Lorraine.

Provençal Tart

1 Roll out the puff pastry on a lightly floured work surface and then use to line a 20-cm/8-inch loose-bottomed quiche/flan tin. Leave to chill in the refrigerator for 20 minutes.

2 Heat 2 tablespoons of the olive oil in a frying pan over a low heat. Add the peppers and fry, stirring frequently, for about 8 minutes or until softened.

3 Whisk the cream and egg together in a bowl and season to taste with salt and pepper. Stir in the cooked peppers.

4 Heat the remaining olive oil in a frying pan over a medium heat. Add the courgette slices and fry, stirring frequently, for 4–5 minutes until browned.

5 Pour the egg and pepper mixture into the pastry case.

6 Arrange the courgette slices around the edge of the tart.

7 Bake in a preheated oven, 180°C/350°F/Gas Mark 4, for 35–40 minutes or until just set and golden-brown. Serve immediately or cool in the tin.

SERVES 6

250 g/9 oz fresh ready-made puff pastry
plain flour, for dusting
3 tbsp olive oil
2 red peppers, deseeded and diced
2 green peppers, deseeded and diced
150 ml/5 fl oz double cream
1 egg
2 courgettes, sliced
salt and pepper

NUTRITION

Calories 355; Sugars 5 g; Protein 5 g; Carbohydrate 21 g; Fat 29 g; Saturates 9 g

   easy

10 mins

55 mins

🥄 **COOK'S TIP**

This recipe could be used to make 6 individual tarts – use 15 x 10-cm/6 x 4-inch tins and bake them for 20 minutes.

This is a French variation of the classic Italian pizza but is made with ready-made puff pastry. It is perfect for outdoor eating.

Pissaladière

SERVES 8

1 tbsp butter, for greasing
4 tbsp olive oil
700 g/1 lb 9 oz red onions, sliced thinly
2 garlic cloves, crushed
2 tsp caster sugar
2 tbsp red wine vinegar
350 g/12 oz fresh ready-made puff pastry
salt and pepper

topping
100 g/3½ oz canned anchovy fillets
12 stoned green olives
1 tsp dried marjoram

1 Lightly grease a Swiss roll tin with the butter. Heat the olive oil in a large, heavy-based saucepan over a low heat. Add the onions and garlic and cook for about 30 minutes, stirring occasionally.

2 Add the sugar and red wine vinegar to the pan and season with plenty of salt and pepper.

3 Roll out the pastry on a lightly floured work surface, to a rectangle about 33 x 23 cm/13 x 9 inches. Transfer the pastry rectangle to the prepared tin, pushing the pastry well into the corners.

4 Spread the onion mixture evenly over the pastry.

5 Drain then arrange the anchovy fillets in a criss-cross pattern on top, place the green olives in between the anchovies, then sprinkle with the marjoram.

6 Bake in a preheated oven, 220°C/425°F/Gas Mark 7, for 20–25 minutes until the pissaladière is lightly golden. Serve piping hot, straight from the oven.

NUTRITION
Calories *290*; Sugars *7 g*; Protein *7 g*;
Carbohydrate *25 g*; Fat *19 g*; Saturates *1 g*

moderate

10 mins

55 mins

🍳 **COOK'S TIP**

Cut the baked pissaladière into squares or triangles for easy finger food at a party or barbecue.

These pretty lattice pies are equally delicious served hot or cold. They make a good picnic food served with salad.

Ham *and* Cheese Lattice Pies

1 Grease 2 baking trays with the butter.

2 Roll out the pastry thinly on a lightly floured work surface and cut out 12 rectangles, each measuring 15 x 5 cm/6 x 2 inches. Place the rectangles on the prepared baking trays and leave to chill in the refrigerator for about 30 minutes.

3 Meanwhile, mix the ham, soft cheese and chives together in a small bowl. Season with pepper to taste, then spread the mixture along the centre of 6 of the rectangles, leaving a 2.5-cm/1-inch border around each one. Brush the border with the beaten egg.

4 To make the lattice pattern, fold the remaining rectangles lengthways, then, leaving a 2.5-cm/1-inch border, cut vertical lines across the folded edge.

5 Unfold the latticed rectangles and place them over the rectangles topped with the ham and cheese mixture. Seal the pastry edges well and sprinkle with the Parmesan cheese. Bake in a preheated oven, 180°C/350°F/Gas Mark 4, for 15–20 minutes. Serve hot or cold.

SERVES 6

2 tbsp butter, for greasing
250 g/9 oz fresh ready-made puff pastry
50 g/1¾ oz ham, chopped finely
125 g/4½ oz full-fat soft cheese
2 tbsp snipped fresh chives
1 egg, beaten
35 g/1¼ oz freshly grated Parmesan cheese
pepper

NUTRITION
Calories 257; Sugars 1 g; Protein 8 g;
Carbohydrate 16 g; Fat 19 g; Saturates 5 g

 moderate

 45 mins

45 mins

20 mins

COOK'S TIP

These pies can be made in advance, then frozen uncooked and baked fresh when required.

Savoury Meals

This chapter presents a mouth-watering array of savoury dishes to tempt any palate, including pies, pastries, tarts and flans, as well as a variety of delicious savoury bakes. The choice is huge, including Cheese Pudding, Red Onion Tart Tatin and Asparagus and Cheese Tart. Fish fans can choose from a wide menu, including Smoky Fish Pie, Seafood Lasagne, and Fillets of Red Mullet and Pasta. Meat and poultry dishes include Parma-Wrapped Chicken, Rich Beef Stew and Italian Chicken Parcels.

This savoury cheese pudding is very like a soufflé in texture, but it does not rise like a traditional soufflé.

Cheese Pudding

SERVES 4

1 tbsp butter, for greasing
150 g/5½ oz fresh white breadcrumbs
100 g/3½ oz Gruyère cheese, grated
150 ml/5 fl oz hand-hot milk
125 g/4½ oz butter, melted
2 eggs, separated
2 tbsp chopped fresh parsley
salt and pepper

1 Grease a 1.2-litre/2-pint ovenproof dish with butter.

2 Mix the breadcrumbs and cheese together in a bowl. Pour over the milk and stir to mix. Add the melted butter, egg yolks, parsley and salt and pepper to taste. Mix well.

3 Whisk the egg whites in a clean bowl until firm, but not stiff. Gently fold the cheese mixture into the egg whites in a figure-of-eight movement.

4 Transfer the mixture to the prepared ovenproof dish and gently smooth the surface with a palette knife.

5 Bake in a preheated oven, 190°C/375°F/Gas Mark 5, for 45 minutes or until golden and slightly risen, and a fine skewer inserted into the centre of the pudding comes out clean. Serve hot.

NUTRITION
Calories *483*; Sugars *3 g*; Protein *15 g*;
Carbohydrate *20 g*; Fat *39 g*; Saturates *24 g*

easy

10 mins

45 mins

👨‍🍳 **COOK'S TIP**

For a slightly healthier alternative, make the cheese pudding with fresh wholemeal breadcrumbs instead of the white breadcrumbs.

Ready-made puff pastry works well in this recipe and means you can create a wonderful savoury tart in very little time.

Red Onion Tart Tatin

1 Place the butter and sugar in a 23-cm/9-inch ovenproof frying pan and cook over a medium heat until melted and combined.

2 Add the red onion quarters and leave them to sweat over a low heat, stirring occasionally, for 10–15 minutes or until golden and caramelized.

3 Add the vinegar and thyme leaves to the pan. Season to taste with salt and pepper, then simmer over a medium heat until the liquid has reduced and the red onion pieces are coated in the buttery sauce.

4 Roll out the pastry on a lightly floured work surface to a circle slightly larger than the frying pan. Place the pastry over the onion mixture in the pan and press down, carefully tucking in the edges to seal it.

5 Bake in a preheated oven, 180°C/350°F/Gas Mark 4, for 20–25 minutes until the pastry is firm and golden-brown. Remove the tart from the oven and leave to stand for 10 minutes.

6 To turn out, place a serving plate over the frying pan and, holding them firmly together, carefully invert them both so that the pastry becomes the base of the tart. Serve warm.

COOK'S TIP

Replace the red onions with shallots, leaving them whole, if you prefer.

SERVES 4

4 tbsp butter
6 tsp sugar
500 g/1 lb 2 oz red onions, quartered
3 tbsp red wine vinegar
2 tbsp fresh thyme leaves
250 g/9 oz fresh ready-made puff pastry
salt and pepper

NUTRITION

Calories *398*; Sugars *14 g*; Protein *5 g*; Carbohydrate *40 g*; Fat *25 g*; Saturates *7 g*

 moderate

 15 mins

50 mins

Fresh asparagus is now readily available all year round, so you can make this tasty and attractive supper dish at any time.

Asparagus *and* Cheese Tart

SERVES 6

250 g/9 oz fresh ready-made shortcrust pastry
250 g/9 oz asparagus
1 tbsp vegetable oil
1 red onion, chopped finely
25 g/1 oz hazelnuts, chopped
200 g/7 oz goat's cheese
2 eggs, beaten
4 tbsp single cream
salt and pepper

1 Roll out the pastry on a lightly floured work surface and use it to line a 24-cm/9½-inch loose-bottomed quiche/flan tin. Prick the base of the pastry with a fork and leave to chill in the refrigerator for 30 minutes.

2 Line the pastry case with foil and baking beans and bake in a preheated oven, 190°C/375°F/Gas Mark 5, for about 15 minutes.

3 Remove the foil and baking beans and cook for a further 15 minutes.

4 Cook the asparagus in boiling water for 2–3 minutes, drain and cut into bite-sized pieces.

5 Heat the vegetable oil in a small frying pan over a low heat. Add the onion and fry, stirring occasionally, until softened and lightly golden. Spoon the asparagus, onion and hazelnuts into the prepared pastry case.

6 Beat the cheese, eggs and cream together in a small bowl until smooth. Alternatively, process in a blender. Season well with salt and pepper, then pour the mixture over the asparagus, onion and hazelnuts.

7 Bake the tart in the preheated oven for 15–20 minutes or until the cheese filling is just set. Serve warm or cold.

COOK'S TIP

Omit the hazelnuts and sprinkle freshly grated Parmesan cheese over the top of the tart just before cooking in the oven, if you prefer.

NUTRITION

Calories *360*; Sugars *4 g*; Protein *11 g*; Carbohydrate *23 g*; Fat *25 g*; Saturates *10 g*

 easy

5–10 mins

 50 mins

This crisp pastry case is filled with a delicious mixture of onions, bacon and cheese and baked until it melts in the mouth.

Onion Tart

1 Roll out the pastry on a lightly floured work surface and use to line a 24-cm/ 9½-inch loose-bottomed quiche/flan tin.

2 Prick the base of the pastry with a fork and leave to chill in the refrigerator for 30 minutes.

3 Meanwhile, heat the butter in a saucepan over a low heat. Add the bacon and onions and leave them to sweat for about 25 minutes or until tender. If the onion slices begin to brown, add 1 tablespoon of water to the pan.

4 Add the beaten eggs to the onion mixture and stir in the grated cheese and sage. Season to taste with salt and pepper.

5 Spoon the bacon and onion mixture into the prepared pastry case.

6 Bake in a preheated oven, 180°C/350°F/Gas Mark 4, for 20–30 minutes or until the filling has just set and the pastry is crisp and golden.

7 Leave the tart to cool slightly in the tin, then remove from the tin and serve warm or cold.

SERVES 4

250 g/9 oz fresh ready-made shortcrust pastry
3 tbsp butter
75 g/2¾ oz bacon, chopped
700 g/1 lb 9 oz onions, sliced thinly
2 eggs, beaten
50 g/1¾ oz freshly grated Parmesan cheese
1 tsp dried sage
salt and pepper

NUTRITION
Calories *394*; Sugars *7 g*; Protein *27 g*;
Carbohydrate *29 g*; Fat *27 g*; Saturates *12 g*

easy

5 mins

45 mins

COOK'S TIP

For a vegetarian version of this tart, replace the bacon with the same amount of chopped mushrooms.

Pizza means 'pie' in Italian. The fresh bread dough is not difficult to make but it does take a little time.

Pizza Margherita

SERVES 4

pizza dough
15 g/½ oz fresh yeast
½ tsp sugar
6 tbsp hand-hot water
175 g/6 oz plain flour, plus extra for dusting
1 tsp salt
1 tbsp olive oil, plus extra for oiling

topping
400 g/14 oz canned tomatoes, chopped
2 garlic cloves, crushed
2 tsp dried basil
1 tbsp olive oil
2 tbsp tomato purée
100 g/3½ oz mozzarella cheese, diced
35 g/1¼ oz freshly grated Parmesan cheese
salt and pepper

NUTRITION
Calories 456; Sugars 7 g; Protein 16 g;
Carbohydrate 74 g; Fat 13 g; Saturates 5 g

  moderate

  1 hr

45 mins

1 To make the pizza dough, mix the yeast, sugar and 4 tablespoons of the water together in a bowl. Leave in a warm place for 15 minutes until frothy.

2 Mix the flour and salt together in a separate bowl and make a well in the centre. Add the olive oil, yeast mixture and remaining water and mix to form a smooth dough.

3 Knead the dough on a floured work surface for 4–5 minutes or until smooth and elastic.

4 Return the dough to the bowl, cover with an oiled sheet of clingfilm and leave to rise for 30 minutes or until doubled in size.

5 Knead the dough for 2 minutes. Stretch it with your hands, then place it on an oiled baking tray, pushing out the edges until it forms a circle. The dough should be no more than 5-mm/¼-inch thick as it will rise during cooking.

6 To make the topping, place the tomatoes, garlic, dried basil and olive oil in a large frying pan and season to taste with salt and pepper. Simmer over a low heat for 20 minutes or until thickened. Stir in the tomato purée, remove from the heat and leave to cool slightly.

7 Spread the topping evenly over the pizza base and top with the mozzarella and Parmesan cheeses. Bake in a preheated oven, 200°C/400°F/Gas Mark 6, for 20–25 minutes until golden. Serve hot.

This is a traditional dish from the Calabrian Mountains in southern Italy, where it is made with sun-dried tomatoes and ricotta cheese.

Tomato *and* Ricotta Pizza

1 Knead the pizza dough on a floured work surface for 2 minutes or until smooth and elastic.

2 Using a rolling pin, roll out the dough to form a circle, then transfer it to a lightly oiled baking tray, pushing out the edges until it forms an even circle. The dough should be no more than about 5-mm/¼-inch thick because it will rise during cooking.

3 Spread the sun-dried tomato paste evenly over the dough, then add spoonfuls of ricotta cheese, dotting them over the top of the pizza.

4 Cut the sun-dried tomatoes into thin strips and arrange these over the top of the pizza.

5 Finally, sprinkle the thyme leaves over the top of the pizza and season to taste with salt and pepper.

6 Bake the pizza in a preheated oven, 200°C/400°F/Gas Mark 6, for 30 minutes or until the crust is golden. Serve hot.

SERVES 4

1 quantity Basic Pizza Dough (see page 15)
plain flour, for dusting
1 tbsp olive oil, for oiling

topping
4 tbsp sun-dried tomato paste
150 g/5½ oz ricotta cheese
10 sun-dried tomatoes bottled in oil, drained
1 tbsp fresh thyme leaves
salt and pepper

NUTRITION
Calories *274*; Sugars *4 g*; Protein *8 g*;
Carbohydrate *38 g*; Fat *11 g*; Saturates *4 g*

 moderate

 1 hr 15 mins

🕐 30 mins

🍳 **COOK'S TIP**

Sun-dried tomatoes are also available in packets. Before using, soak them in hot water until they are soft. Keep the tomato-flavoured soaking water to use in soups or sauces.

This pizza is a favourite in Rome. It is slightly unusual because the topping is made without a tomato sauce base.

Onion, Ham *and* Cheese Pizza

SERVES 4

1 quantity Basic Pizza Dough (see page 15)
plain flour, for dusting
1 tbsp olive oil, for oiling

topping

2 tbsp olive oil
250 g/9 oz onions, sliced into rings
2 garlic cloves, crushed
1 red pepper, deseeded and diced
100 g/3½ oz Parma ham, cut into strips
100 g/3½ oz mozzarella cheese, sliced
2 tbsp fresh rosemary sprigs, stalks removed and roughly chopped

NUTRITION

Calories 333; Sugars 8 g; Protein 12 g;
Carbohydrate 43 g; Fat 14 g; Saturates 4 g

moderate

1 hr

40 mins

1 Knead the pizza dough on a floured work surface for 2 minutes or until smooth and elastic.

2 Using a rolling pin, roll out the dough to form a square shape, then place it on an oiled baking tray, pushing out the edges until even. The dough should be no more than 5-mm/¼-inch thick because it will rise during cooking.

3 To make the topping, heat the olive oil in a heavy-based pan over a low heat. Add the onions and garlic and cook, stirring frequently, for 3 minutes. Add the red pepper and fry, stirring frequently, for 2 minutes.

4 Cover the pan and cook the vegetables over a low heat for about 10 minutes, stirring occasionally, until the onions are slightly caramelized. Remove the pan from the heat and leave to cool slightly.

5 Spread the topping evenly over the pizza base. Arrange the Parma ham, mozzarella and rosemary over the top.

6 Bake in a preheated oven, 200°C/400°F/Gas Mark 6, for 20–25 minutes. Serve the pizza hot.

COOK'S TIP

Parma ham, also known as prosciutto, is a classic, dry-cured, raw Italian ham. Other similar hams include prosciutto di San Daniele and prosciutto Veneto.

This pizza is made with a pastry base flavoured with cheese and topped with a delicious tomato sauce and roasted peppers.

Tomato *and* Pepper Pizza

1 Sift the flour into a bowl. Add the butter and rub it in with your fingertips until the mixture resembles breadcrumbs. Stir in the salt and Parmesan cheese. Add the egg and 1 tablespoon of the water and mix with a round-bladed knife. Add more water if necessary to make a soft dough. Form into a ball, cover with clingfilm and leave to chill in the refrigerator for 30 minutes.

2 Meanwhile, heat the olive oil in a frying pan over a low heat. Add the onion and garlic and cook for about 5 minutes or until golden. Add the chopped tomatoes and cook for 8–10 minutes. Stir in the tomato purée.

3 Place the pepper, skin side up, on a baking tray and cook under a preheated hot grill for 15 minutes until charred. Place in a plastic bag and leave to sweat for 10 minutes. Peel off the skin and slice the flesh into thin strips.

4 Roll out the dough to fit a 23-cm/9-inch loose-bottomed fluted flan tin. Line with foil and bake in a preheated oven, 200°C/400°F/Gas Mark 6, for about 10 minutes or until just set. Remove the foil and bake for a further 5 minutes until lightly golden. Leave to cool slightly.

5 Spoon the tomato sauce over the pastry base and top with the pepper, thyme, olives and fresh Parmesan cheese. Return to the oven for 15 minutes or until the pastry is crisp. Serve warm or cold.

SERVES 4

225 g/8 oz plain flour, plus extra for dusting
125 g/4½ oz butter, diced
½ tsp salt
35 g/1¼ oz ready grated Parmesan cheese
1 egg, beaten
1–2 tbsp cold water
2 tbsp olive oil
1 large onion, chopped finely
1 garlic clove, chopped
400 g/14 oz canned chopped tomatoes
4 tbsp tomato purée
1 red pepper, deseeded and halved
5 fresh thyme sprigs, stalks removed
6 black olives, stoned and halved
25 g/1 oz freshly grated Parmesan cheese

NUTRITION
Calories 611; Sugars 8 g; Protein 14 g; Carbohydrate 56 g; Fat 38 g; Saturates 21 g

★★★   moderate
    1 hr 30 mins
   55 mins

This traditional Easter risotto pie is from Piedmont in northern Italy. Cut into slices and serve it either warm or chilled.

Green Easter Pie

SERVES 4

1 tbsp butter, for greasing
85 g/3 oz rocket leaves
2 tbsp olive oil
1 onion, chopped
2 garlic cloves, chopped
200 g/7 oz arborio rice
700 ml/1¼ pints hot chicken or vegetable stock
125 ml/4 fl oz white wine
50 g/1¾ oz freshly grated Parmesan cheese
100 g/3½ oz frozen peas, thawed
2 tomatoes, diced
4 eggs, beaten
3 tbsp fresh marjoram, chopped
50 g/1¾ oz fresh breadcrumbs
salt and pepper

NUTRITION
Calories 392; Sugars 3 g; Protein 17 g;
Carbohydrate 41 g; Fat 17 g; Saturates 5 g

 moderate

25 mins

50 mins

1 Lightly grease a 23-cm/9-inch deep cake tin with butter and line the base with baking paper.

2 Using a sharp knife, roughly chop the rocket leaves.

3 Heat the olive oil in a frying pan over a low heat. Add the onion and garlic and fry for 4–5 minutes or until softened.

4 Add the rice to the mixture in the frying pan, mix well, then begin adding the stock, a ladleful at a time. Wait until each ladleful of stock has been absorbed before adding the next.

5 Continue to cook the mixture, adding the wine, until the rice is tender. This will take at least 15 minutes. Remove the pan from the heat.

6 Stir in the Parmesan cheese, peas, rocket leaves, tomatoes, eggs and 2 tablespoons of the marjoram. Season to taste with salt and pepper.

7 Spoon the risotto into the prepared tin and smooth the surface by pressing down with the back of a wooden spoon. Top with the breadcrumbs and the remaining marjoram.

8 Bake in a preheated oven, 180°C/350°F/Gas Mark 4, for 30 minutes or until set. Cut into slices and serve.

This puff pastry pie looks impressive, but it is actually fairly easy and quite quick to make. Serve it hot or cold.

Spinach *and* Ricotta Pie

1 Rinse the spinach, place in a large saucepan with just the water clinging to the leaves and cook over a low heat for 4–5 minutes until wilted. Drain thoroughly. When the spinach is cool enough to handle, squeeze out the excess liquid.

2 Place the pine kernels on a baking tray and lightly toast under a preheated hot grill for 2–3 minutes or until golden-brown.

3 Mix the ricotta, spinach and eggs together in a bowl. Add the pine kernels, beat well, then stir in the ground almonds and Parmesan cheese.

4 Roll out the pastry on a lightly floured work surface and make 2 squares, about 20-cm/8-inches wide. Trim the edges, reserving the pastry trimmings.

5 Place 1 pastry square on a baking tray and spoon over the spinach mixture to within 1 cm/½ inch of the edge of the pastry. Brush the edges with beaten egg and place the second square over the top.

6 Using a round-bladed knife, press the pastry edges together by tapping along the sealed edge. Use the pastry trimmings to make a few leaves to decorate the pie.

7 Brush the pie with the beaten egg and bake in a preheated oven, 220°C/425°F/Gas Mark 7, for about 10 minutes. Reduce the oven temperature to 190°C/375°F/Gas Mark 5 and bake for a further 25–30 minutes. Serve hot.

SERVES 4

225 g/8 oz fresh spinach
25 g/1 oz pine kernels
100 g/3½ oz ricotta cheese
2 large eggs, beaten
50 g/1¾ oz ground almonds
40 g/1½ oz freshly grated Parmesan cheese
250 g/9 oz ready-made puff pastry
plain flour, for dusting
1 small egg, beaten

NUTRITION
Calories *545*; Sugars *3 g*; Protein *19 g*;
Carbohydrate *25 g*; Fat *42 g*; Saturates *13 g*

moderate

25 mins

50 mins

Always check the seasoning of vegetables – you can always add a little more to a recipe, but you cannot take it out once it has been added.

Spinach *and* Mushroom Lasagne

SERVES 4

115 g/4 oz butter, plus extra for greasing
2 garlic cloves, chopped finely
115 g/4 oz shallots
225 g/8 oz wild mushrooms, such as chanterelles
450 g/1 lb spinach, cooked, drained and finely chopped
225 g/8 oz Cheddar cheese, grated
¼ tsp freshly grated nutmeg
1 tsp chopped fresh basil
6 tbsp plain flour
600 ml/1 pint hot milk
55 g/2 oz Cheshire cheese, grated
8 sheets precooked lasagne
salt and pepper
salad leaves, to serve

NUTRITION

Calories 720; Sugars 9 g; Protein 31 g;
Carbohydrate 36 g; Fat 52 g; Saturates 32 g

  easy

  20 mins

  40 mins

1 Lightly grease a large, rectangular or square ovenproof dish with butter.

2 Melt 55 g/2 oz of the butter in a frying pan over a low heat. Add the garlic, shallots and wild mushrooms and fry, stirring occasionally, for 3 minutes.

3 Stir in the spinach, Cheddar cheese, nutmeg and basil. Season to taste with salt and pepper, remove from the heat and reserve.

4 Melt the remaining butter in a saucepan over a low heat. Add the flour and cook, stirring constantly, for 1 minute. Gradually stir in the hot milk, whisking constantly, until smooth and thickened. Remove the pan from the heat and stir in 25 g/1 oz of the Cheshire cheese. Season to taste with salt and pepper.

5 Spread half of the mushroom and spinach mixture over the base of the prepared dish. Cover with a layer of lasagne and then with half of the cheese sauce. Repeat the layers and sprinkle the remaining grated Cheshire cheese over the top.

6 Bake in a preheated oven, 200°C/400°F/Gas Mark 6, for 30 minutes or until golden-brown. Serve hot with salad leaves.

COOK'S TIP

You could substitute 4 peppers for the spinach. Roast them in a preheated oven, 200°C/400°F/Gas Mark 6, for 20 minutes. Rub off the skins under cold water, deseed and chop before using.

It is important not to overcook the vegetable filling or it will become sloppy and unexciting, instead of firm to the bite and delicious.

Vegetable Ravioli

1 To make the stuffing, cut the aubergines and the courgettes into 2.5-cm/ 1-inch chunks. Place the aubergine pieces in layers in a colander, sprinkle each layer with salt and set aside for 20 minutes. Rinse and drain, then pat dry on kitchen paper.

2 Blanch the tomatoes in boiling water for 2 minutes. Drain, peel and chop the flesh. Core and deseed the peppers and cut into 2.5-cm/1-inch dice. Chop the garlic and onion.

3 Heat the olive oil in a saucepan over a low heat. Add the garlic and onion and fry, stirring occasionally, for 3 minutes. Stir in the aubergines, courgettes, tomatoes, peppers, tomato purée and basil. Season to taste with salt and pepper, cover and simmer for 20 minutes, stirring frequently.

4 Roll out the pasta dough on a lightly floured work surface and cut out 7.5-cm/3-inch rounds with a plain cutter. Put a spoonful of the vegetable stuffing on each round. Dampen the edges slightly and fold the pasta rounds over, pressing together to seal.

5 Bring a large saucepan of lightly salted water to the boil over a medium heat. Add the ravioli and olive oil and cook for 3–4 minutes. Drain and transfer to a greased ovenproof dish, dotting each layer with butter. Pour over the cream and sprinkle over the Parmesan cheese. Bake in a preheated oven, 200°C/400°F/Gas Mark 6, for 20 minutes. Garnish with a few sprigs of fresh basil and serve hot.

SERVES 4

450 g/1 lb Basic Pasta Dough (see page 15)
plain flour, for dusting
1 tbsp olive oil
6 tbsp butter, plus extra for greasing
150 ml/5 fl oz single cream
85 g/3 oz freshly grated Parmesan cheese
fresh basil sprigs, to garnish

stuffing

2 large aubergines
3 large courgettes
6 large tomatoes
1 large green pepper
1 large red pepper
3 garlic cloves
1 large onion
125 ml/4 fl oz olive oil
4½ tsp tomato purée
½ tsp chopped fresh basil
salt and pepper

NUTRITION
Calories *622*; Sugars *10 g*; Protein *12 g*;
Carbohydrate *58 g*; Fat *40 g*; Saturates *6 g*

 challenging

 1 hr 30 mins

55 mins

This rich, baked pasta dish is packed full of vegetables, tomatoes and Italian mozzarella cheese and makes a delightful change.

Vegetable Lasagne

SERVES 6

1 kg/2 lb 4 oz aubergines
125 ml/4 fl oz olive oil
2 tbsp garlic and herb butter
450 g/1 lb courgettes, sliced
225 g/8 oz mozzarella cheese, grated
600 ml/1 pint passata
6 sheets precooked green lasagne
600 ml/1 pint Béchamel Sauce (see page 73)
55 g/2 oz freshly grated Parmesan cheese
1 tsp dried oregano
salt and pepper

NUTRITION
Calories 510; Sugars 14 g; Protein 17 g;
Carbohydrate 28 g; Fat 38 g; Saturates 14 g

 moderate

 50 mins

50 mins

1 Thinly slice the aubergines and place in layers in a colander. Sprinkle each layer with salt and set aside for 20 minutes. Rinse and drain, then pat dry on kitchen paper.

2 Heat 4 tablespoons of the olive oil in a large, heavy-based frying pan over a low heat. Add half the aubergine slices and fry for 6–7 minutes or until golden. Drain thoroughly on kitchen paper. Repeat with the remaining olive oil and aubergine slices.

3 Melt the garlic and herb butter in the frying pan over a medium heat. Add the courgettes and fry, stirring occasionally, for 5–6 minutes until golden-brown all over. Drain thoroughly on kitchen paper.

4 Place half of the aubergine and courgette slices in a large ovenproof dish. Season to taste with pepper and sprinkle over half of the grated mozzarella cheese. Spoon over half of the passata and top with 3 sheets of lasagne. Repeat the layering process, ending with a layer of lasagne sheets.

5 Spoon over the béchamel sauce and sprinkle the Parmesan cheese and oregano over the top. Put the dish on a baking tray and bake in a preheated oven, 220°C/425°F/Gas Mark 7, for 30–35 minutes or until golden-brown. Serve immediately.

Combined with tomatoes and melting mozzarella cheese, pasta makes a tasty filling for baked aubergine shells.

Filled Aubergines

1 Bring a large saucepan of lightly salted water to the boil over a medium heat. Add the penne and 1 tablespoon of the olive oil, bring back to the boil and cook for 8–10 minutes or until just tender, but still firm to the bite. Drain, return to the pan, cover and keep warm.

2 Cut the aubergines in half lengthways and score around the inside with a sharp knife, being careful not to pierce the shells. Scoop out the flesh with a spoon, then brush the insides of the shells with a little olive oil. Chop the flesh and reserve.

3 Heat the remaining olive oil in a frying pan over a medium heat. Add the onion and fry until translucent. Add the garlic and fry for 1 minute. Add the chopped aubergine flesh and fry, stirring frequently, for 5 minutes. Add the tomatoes and oregano and season to taste with salt and pepper. Bring to the boil and simmer for 10 minutes, or until thickened. Remove the pan from the heat and stir in the pasta.

4 Brush a baking tray with olive oil and arrange the aubergine shells in a single layer. Divide half of the tomato and pasta mixture between them. Scatter over the mozzarella cheese, then pile the remaining tomato and pasta mixture on top. Mix the Parmesan cheese and breadcrumbs together and sprinkle over the top, patting it lightly into the mixture.

5 Bake in a preheated oven, 200°C/400°C/Gas Mark 6, for about 25 minutes or until the topping is golden-brown. Serve hot with salad leaves.

SERVES 4

225 g/8 oz dried penne or other short pasta shapes
4 tbsp olive oil, plus extra for brushing
2 aubergines
1 large onion, chopped
2 garlic cloves, crushed
400 g/14 oz canned chopped tomatoes
2 tsp dried oregano
55 g/2 oz mozzarella cheese, sliced thinly
25 g/1 oz freshly grated Parmesan cheese
25 g/1 oz dry breadcrumbs
salt and pepper
salad leaves, to serve

NUTRITION
Calories 342; Sugars 6 g; Protein 11 g; Carbohydrate 40 g; Fat 16 g; Saturates 4 g

moderate

25 mins

55 mins

This adaptation of an 18th-century Italian dish is baked until it is golden-brown and sizzling, then cut into wedges, like a cake.

Macaroni *and* Prawn Bake

SERVES 4

350 g/12 oz dried short pasta shapes, such as short-cut macaroni
1 tbsp olive oil, plus extra for brushing
6 tbsp butter, plus extra for greasing
2 small fennel bulbs, sliced thinly, leaves reserved
175 g/6 oz mushrooms, sliced thinly
175 g/6 oz cooked, peeled prawns, thawed if frozen
600 ml/1 pint Béchamel Sauce (see page 73)
pinch of cayenne pepper
55 g/2 oz freshly grated Parmesan cheese
2 large tomatoes, sliced
1 tsp dried oregano
salt
4 fresh flat-leaf parsley sprigs, to garnish

NUTRITION

Calories *576*; Sugars *6 g*; Protein *25 g*; Carbohydrate *42 g*; Fat *35 g*; Saturates *19 g*

 moderate

 20 mins

20 mins

1 hr 5 mins

1 Bring a large saucepan of lightly salted water to the boil over a medium heat. Add the pasta and 1 tablespoon of olive oil, bring back to the boil and cook for 8–10 minutes or until just tender, but still firm to the bite. Drain, return to the pan and dot with 2 tablespoons of the butter. Shake the pan well to coat the pasta, cover and keep warm.

2 Melt the remaining butter in a large saucepan over a medium heat. Add the fennel and fry for 3–4 minutes, stirring occasionally, until it begins to soften. Stir in the mushrooms and stir-fry for 2 minutes. Stir in the prawns, remove the pan from the heat and reserve until required.

3 Make the béchamel sauce and season to taste with cayenne. Remove the pan from the heat and stir in the reserved vegetable and prawn mixture and the pasta.

4 Grease a round, shallow ovenproof dish with butter. Pour in the pasta mixture and spread evenly. Sprinkle with Parmesan cheese and arrange the tomato slices in a ring around the edge of the dish. Brush the tomato slices with olive oil and sprinkle with the dried oregano.

5 Bake in a preheated oven, 180°C/350°F/Gas Mark 4, for 25 minutes or until golden-brown. Transfer to 4 warmed serving plates, garnish with sprigs of fresh parsley and serve hot.

You can use any fish and any sauce you like in this recipe: try smoked finnan haddock and whisky sauce or cod with cheese sauce.

Seafood Lasagne

1 Put the haddock fillet, prawns and sole fillet into a large bowl and season with pepper and lemon juice according to taste. Cover and reserve while you make the sauce.

2 Melt the butter in a large saucepan over a low heat. Add the leeks and cook, stirring occasionally, for 8 minutes until softened. Add the flour and cook, stirring constantly, for 1 minute. Gradually stir in enough milk to make a thick, creamy sauce.

3 Blend in the honey and mozzarella cheese and cook for a further 3 minutes. Remove the pan from the heat and mix in the fish and prawns.

4 Grease a large ovenproof dish with butter. Make alternate layers of fish sauce and lasagne, finishing with a layer of fish sauce on top. Sprinkle over the Parmesan cheese and bake in a preheated oven, 180°C/350°F/Gas Mark 4, for 30 minutes. Serve immediately.

SERVES 4

450 g/1 lb finnan haddock fillet, skin removed and flesh sliced
115 g/4 oz raw prawns, peeled
115 g/4 oz sole fillet, skin removed and flesh sliced
juice of 1 lemon
4 tbsp butter, plus extra for greasing
3 leeks, sliced very thinly
6 tbsp plain flour
about 600 ml/1 pint milk
2 tbsp clear honey
200 g/7 oz mozzarella cheese, grated
450 g/1 lb precooked lasagne
55 g/2 oz freshly grated Parmesan cheese
pepper

NUTRITION
Calories 790; Sugars 23 g; Protein 55 g; Carbohydrate 74 g; Fat 32 g; Saturates 19 g

 moderate
 30 mins
30 mins
45 mins

👨‍🍳 COOK'S TIP

To make a cider sauce, substitute 1 finely chopped shallot for the leeks, 300 ml/10 fl oz cider and 300 ml/10 fl oz double cream for the milk and 1 teaspoon mustard for the honey.

This flavoursome and colourful fish pie is perfect for a light supper. The addition of smoked salmon gives it a touch of luxury.

Smoky Fish Pie

SERVES 4

900 g/2 lb smoked haddock or cod fillets
600 ml/1 pint skimmed milk
2 bay leaves
115 g/4 oz button mushrooms, quartered
115 g/4 oz frozen peas
115 g/4 oz frozen sweetcorn kernels
650 g/1 lb 7 oz potatoes, peeled and diced
5 tbsp low-fat natural yogurt
4 tbsp chopped fresh parsley
55 g/2 oz smoked salmon, sliced into thin strips
3 tbsp cornflour
25 g/1 oz smoked cheese, grated
salt and pepper

NUTRITION

Calories 523; Sugars 15 g; Protein 58 g;
Carbohydrate 63 g; Fat 6 g; Saturates 2 g

  moderate

  15 mins

🕐 1 hr

1 Place the fish in a large frying pan and add the milk and bay leaves. Bring to the boil over a medium heat, cover and simmer for 5 minutes. Add the mushrooms, peas and sweetcorn, bring back to a simmer, cover and cook for 5–7 minutes. Leave to cool.

2 Place the potatoes in a saucepan, cover with water, bring to the boil over a medium heat and cook for 8 minutes. Drain well and mash with a fork. Stir in the yogurt and parsley and season to taste with salt and pepper. Reserve.

3 Using a slotted spoon, remove the fish from the pan. Flake the cooked fish away from the skin and place in an ovenproof dish. Reserve the cooking liquid. Drain the vegetables, reserving the cooking liquid, and gently stir into the fish with the salmon strips.

4 Blend the cornflour with a little cooking liquid to make a paste. Transfer the rest of the liquid to a saucepan and add the paste. Heat through, stirring, until thickened. Remove and discard the bay leaves and season to taste. Pour the sauce over the fish and vegetables and mix. Spoon over the mashed potato to cover, sprinkle with the grated cheese and bake in a preheated oven, 200°C/400°F/Gas Mark 6, for about 25–30 minutes. Serve hot.

👑 COOK'S TIP

If possible, use smoked haddock or cod that has not been dyed bright yellow or artificially flavoured to give the illusion of having been smoked.

This dish is ideal for a substantial supper. You can use whatever pasta you like, but the tricolour varieties will give the most colourful results.

Prawn Pasta Bake

1 Bring a large saucepan of lightly salted water to the boil over a medium heat. Add the pasta, bring back to the boil and cook for 8–10 minutes or until tender, but still firm to the bite. Drain well and reserve.

2 Meanwhile, heat the vegetable oil in a large frying pan over a low heat. Add the mushrooms and all but a handful of the spring onions and cook, stirring occasionally, for 4–5 minutes until softened.

3 Place the cooked pasta in a bowl and stir in the mushroom mixture, tuna and prawns.

4 Blend the cornflour with a little milk to make a paste. Transfer the rest of the milk to a saucepan and stir in the paste. Heat, stirring constantly, until the sauce begins to thicken. Season well with salt and pepper. Add the sauce to the pasta mixture and mix thoroughly. Transfer to an ovenproof dish and place on a baking tray.

5 Arrange the tomato slices over the pasta and sprinkle with the breadcrumbs and cheese. Bake in a preheated oven, 190°C/375°F/Gas Mark 5, for about 25–30 minutes until golden. Sprinkle with the reserved spring onions and serve hot.

SERVES 4

225 g/8 oz dried tricolour pasta shapes
1 tbsp vegetable oil
175 g/6 oz button mushrooms, sliced
1 bunch spring onions, trimmed and chopped
400 g/14 oz canned tuna in brine, drained and flaked
175 g/6 oz peeled prawns, thawed if frozen
2 tbsp cornflour
425 ml/15 fl oz skimmed milk
4 medium tomatoes, sliced thinly
25 g/1 oz fresh breadcrumbs
25 g/1 oz reduced-fat Cheddar cheese, grated
salt and pepper

NUTRITION
Calories 723; Sugars 9 g; Protein 56 g; Carbohydrate 114 g; Fat 8 g; Saturates 2 g

✪✪✪   moderate

🟢   10 mins

🔵   50 mins

Using polenta as a crust for a gratin dish gives a lovely crispy outer texture and a smooth inside. It works very well with smoked fish and chicken.

Smoked Cod Polenta

SERVES 4

1.5 litres/2¾ pints water
350 g/12 oz instant polenta
200 g/7 oz chopped frozen spinach, thawed
3 tbsp butter
50 g/1¾ oz pecorino cheese, grated
200 ml/7 fl oz milk
450 g/1 lb smoked cod fillet, skinned and boned
4 eggs, beaten
salt and pepper

1 Bring the water to the boil in a large saucepan over a medium heat. Add the polenta and cook, stirring constantly, for 30–35 minutes.

2 Stir the spinach, butter and half of the pecorino cheese into the polenta. Season to taste with salt and pepper.

3 Divide the cooked polenta between 4 individual ovenproof dishes, spreading it evenly across the bases and up the sides of the dishes.

4 Bring the milk to the boil in a frying pan over a low heat. Add the fish and cook, turning once, for 8–10 minutes or until the flesh is tender and flakes easily with a fork. Remove the fish carefully with a slotted spoon.

5 Remove the pan from the heat. Pour the eggs into the milk in the pan and mix together.

6 Using a fork, flake the fish into smaller pieces and place it in the centre of the dishes, then pour the milk and egg mixture over the fish.

7 Sprinkle with the remaining cheese and bake in a preheated oven, 190°C/375°F/Gas Mark 5, for 25–30 minutes or until set and golden. Serve hot.

NUTRITION

Calories *616*; Sugars *3 g*; Protein *41 g*; Carbohydrate *58 g*; Fat *24 g*; Saturates *12 g*

moderate

30 mins

1 hr 15 mins

🍳 **COOK'S TIP**

Try using 350 g/12 oz cooked chicken breast with 2 tablespoons of chopped fresh tarragon, instead of the smoked cod, if you prefer.

Cod roasted with herbs and topped with a lemon and rosemary crust is a delicious main course that is perfect for a warm, summer's evening.

Italian Cod

1 Melt the butter in a large saucepan over a low heat.

2 Remove the pan from the heat and add the breadcrumbs, walnuts, the rind and juice of 1 lemon, half of the rosemary and half of the parsley.

3 Gently press the breadcrumb mixture over the top of the cod fillets. Place the cod fillets in a shallow, foil-lined roasting tin.

4 Bake in a preheated oven, 200°C/400°F/Gas Mark 6, for 25–30 minutes.

5 Mix the garlic, the remaining lemon rind and juice, rosemary, parsley and chilli together in a bowl. Beat in the walnut oil and mix well. Drizzle the dressing over the cod fillets as soon as they are cooked.

6 Transfer the fish to 4 serving plates and serve with mixed salad leaves.

SERVES 4

2 tbsp butter
50 g/1¾ oz wholemeal breadcrumbs
25 g/1 oz chopped walnuts
grated rind and juice of 2 lemons
2 fresh rosemary sprigs, stalks removed
2 tbsp chopped fresh parsley
4 cod fillets, about 150 g/5½ oz each
1 garlic clove, crushed
1 small fresh red chilli, deseeded and diced
3 tbsp walnut oil
mixed salad leaves, to serve

NUTRITION
Calories 313; Sugars 0.4 g; Protein 29 g; Carbohydrate 6 g; Fat 20 g; Saturates 5 g

 easy

 10 mins

🕐 35 mins

🍴 **COOK'S TIP**

If preferred, the walnuts may be omitted from the crust. In addition, extra virgin olive oil can be used instead of walnut oil, if you prefer.

This is a lighter dish than the better-known cannelloni filled with beef and would be ideal for an informal dinner party.

Cannelloni Filetti *di* Sogliola

SERVES 6

12 small sole fillets, about 115 g/4 oz each
150 ml/5 fl oz red wine
6 tbsp butter
115 g/4 oz sliced button mushrooms
4 shallots, chopped finely
115 g/4 oz tomatoes, chopped
2 tbsp tomato purée
6 tbsp plain flour, sifted
150 ml/5 fl oz warm milk
2 tbsp double cream
6 dried cannelloni tubes
175 g/6 oz cooked, peeled prawns, preferably freshwater
salt and pepper
1 fresh fennel frond, to garnish

NUTRITION

Calories 555; Sugars 4 g; Protein 53 g; Carbohydrate 36 g; Fat 21 g; Saturates 12 g

challenging

20 mins

45 mins

1 Brush the sole fillets with a little wine, season with salt and pepper and roll them up, skin side inwards. Secure with a skewer or cocktail stick.

2 Place the fish rolls in a single layer in a large frying pan, add the remaining red wine and poach for 4 minutes. Remove the fish from the pan and reserve the liquid.

3 Melt the butter in a separate large frying pan over a low heat. Add the mushrooms and shallots and fry for 2 minutes, then add the tomatoes and tomato purée. Season the flour and stir it into the pan. Stir in the reserved cooking liquid and half the milk. Cook, stirring constantly, for 4 minutes. Remove from the heat and stir in the cream.

4 Bring a large saucepan of lightly salted water to the boil over a medium heat. Add the cannelloni, bring back to the boil and cook for 8 minutes or until just tender, but still firm to the bite. Drain and leave to cool.

5 Remove the skewers or cocktail sticks from the fish rolls. Put 2 sole fillets into each cannelloni tube together with 2–3 prawns and a little red wine sauce. Arrange the cannelloni in a single layer in a large ovenproof dish, pour over the red wine sauce and bake in a preheated oven, 200°C/400°F/Gas Mark 6, for 20 minutes or until cooked through and piping hot.

6 Serve the cannelloni immediately with the red wine sauce, garnished with the remaining prawns and a frond of fresh fennel.

This simple recipe perfectly complements the wonderfully sweet flavour and delicate texture of the fish.

Fillets *of* Red Mullet *and* Pasta

1 Place the red mullet fillets in a large casserole. Pour over the wine and add the shallots, garlic, herbs, lemon rind and juice, nutmeg and anchovies. Season to taste with salt and pepper. Cover and bake in a preheated oven, 180°C/350°F/Gas Mark 4, for 35 minutes.

2 Transfer the red mullet to a warmed dish. Cover lightly and keep warm.

3 Pour the cooking liquid into a small saucepan and bring to the boil over a medium heat. Simmer for 25 minutes until reduced by half. Mix the cream and cornflour together and stir into the sauce to thicken.

4 Meanwhile, bring a large saucepan of lightly salted water to the boil over a medium heat. Add the vermicelli and olive oil, bring back to the boil and cook for 8–10 minutes or until tender, but still firm to the bite. Drain the pasta and transfer to 4 warmed serving dishes.

5 Arrange the red mullet fillets on top of the vermicelli and pour over the sauce. Garnish with fresh mint sprigs, slices of lemon and strips of lemon rind and serve immediately.

SERVES 4

1 kg/2 lb 4 oz red mullet fillets
300 ml/10 fl oz dry white wine
4 shallots, chopped finely
1 garlic clove, crushed
3 tbsp finely chopped mixed fresh herbs
finely grated rind and juice of 1 lemon
pinch of freshly grated nutmeg
3 anchovy fillets, chopped roughly
2 tbsp double cream
1 tsp cornflour
450 g/1 lb dried vermicelli
1 tbsp olive oil
salt and pepper

to garnish
4 fresh mint sprigs
lemon slices
strips of lemon rind

NUTRITION
Calories *457*; Sugars *3 g*; Protein *39 g*;
Carbohydrate *44 g*; Fat *12 g*; Saturates *5 g*

★★★ moderate

 15 mins

1 hr

Most trout available nowadays is farmed rainbow trout. However, if you can, buy the superb-tasting wild brown trout for this recipe.

Trout *with* Smoked Bacon

SERVES 4

1 tbsp butter, for greasing
4 whole trout, about 275 g/9½ oz each, cleaned and rinsed
12 anchovies in oil, drained and chopped
2 apples, peeled, cored and sliced
4 fresh mint sprigs
juice of 1 lemon
12 slices rindless smoked streaky bacon
450 g/1 lb dried tagliatelle
1 tbsp olive oil
salt and pepper

to garnish
2 apples, cored and sliced
4 fresh mint sprigs

NUTRITION
Calories *802*; Sugars *8 g*; Protein *68 g*;
Carbohydrate *54 g*; Fat *36 g*; Saturates *10 g*

⭐⭐⭐⭐ challenging

 35 mins

🕐 30 mins

1 Grease a deep baking tray with the butter.

2 Open up the cavities of each trout and rinse with warm salt water.

3 Season each cavity with salt and pepper. Divide the anchovies, sliced apples and mint sprigs between each of the cavities. Sprinkle with lemon juice.

4 Cover the whole of each trout, except the head and tail, with 3 slices of smoked bacon in a spiral.

5 Arrange the trout on the prepared baking tray with the loose ends of bacon tucked underneath. Season to taste with pepper and bake in a preheated oven, 200°C/400°F/Gas Mark 6, for 20 minutes, turning the trout over after 10 minutes.

6 Meanwhile, bring a large saucepan of lightly salted water to the boil over a medium heat. Add the tagliatelle and olive oil and cook for 12 minutes or until tender, but still firm to the bite. Drain and transfer to a large, warmed serving dish.

7 Remove the trout from the oven and arrange on the tagliatelle. Garnish with sliced apples and fresh mint sprigs and serve immediately.

This quick, easy and inexpensive dish would be ideal for a mid-week family supper, as it is both nourishing and filling.

Smoked Haddock Casserole

1 Grease a large casserole with butter. Place the haddock in the casserole and pour over the milk. Bake in a preheated oven, 200°C/400°F/Gas Mark 6, for about 15 minutes or until the flesh is tender and flakes easily with a fork. Carefully pour the cooking liquid into a jug without breaking up the fish.

2 Melt the butter in a saucepan over a low heat and stir in the flour. Gradually whisk in the reserved cooking liquid. Season to taste with salt, pepper and nutmeg. Stir in the cream, parsley and mashed hard-boiled egg and cook, stirring constantly, for 2 minutes.

3 Meanwhile, bring a large saucepan of lightly salted water to the boil over a medium heat. Add the fusilli and lemon juice, bring back to the boil and cook for 8–10 minutes or until tender, but still firm to the bite.

4 Drain the pasta and spoon or tip it over the fish. Top with the egg sauce and return the casserole to the oven for 10 minutes.

5 Transfer the casserole to 4 warmed serving plates and garnish with sprigs of fresh parsley. Serve with boiled new potatoes and beetroot.

SERVES 4

2 tbsp butter, plus extra for greasing
450 g/1 lb smoked haddock fillets, cut into 4 slices
600 ml/1 pint milk
2½ tbsp plain flour
pinch of freshly grated nutmeg
3 tbsp double cream
1 tbsp chopped fresh parsley
2 eggs, hard-boiled and mashed to a pulp
450 g/1 lb dried fusilli
1 tbsp lemon juice
salt and pepper
4 fresh flat-leaf parsley sprigs, to garnish

to serve
boiled new potatoes
freshly cooked slices of beetroot

NUTRITION
Calories *525*; Sugars *8 g*; Protein *41 g*; Carbohydrate *53 g*; Fat *18 g*; Saturates *10 g*

 moderate

 20 mins

  45 mins

🍳 **COOK'S TIP**

You can use any type of dried pasta for this casserole. Try penne, conchiglie, farfalle or rigatoni.

This recipe is a type of cottage pie and is just as versatile. Add vegetables and herbs of your choice, depending on what you have at hand.

Quick Chicken Bake

SERVES 4

500 g/1 lb 2 oz fresh chicken mince
1 large onion, chopped finely
2 carrots, diced finely
25 g/1 oz plain flour
1 tbsp tomato purée
300 ml/10 fl oz chicken stock
pinch of fresh thyme
900 g/2 lb boiled potatoes, creamed with butter and milk and highly seasoned
85 g/3 oz Lancashire cheese, grated
salt and pepper
freshly cooked peas, to serve

1 Dry-fry the chicken mince, onion and carrots in a non-stick saucepan over a low heat, stirring frequently, for about 5 minutes until the chicken is completely sealed.

2 Sprinkle the chicken with the flour and cook, stirring constantly, for a further 2 minutes.

3 Gradually blend in the tomato purée and stock, then simmer for 15 minutes. Season to taste with salt and pepper and add the thyme.

4 Transfer the chicken and vegetable mixture to a large casserole and leave to cool completely.

5 Spoon the creamed potato over the chicken mixture and sprinkle with the grated cheese. Bake in a preheated oven, 200°C/400°F/Gas Mark 6, for about 20 minutes, or until the cheese is bubbling and golden. Serve immediately with freshly cooked peas.

NUTRITION
Calories 530; Sugars 8 g; Protein 37 g;
Carbohydrate 48 g; Fat 23 g; Saturates 12 g

 moderate

 1 hr 45 mins

45 mins

🍳 **COOK'S TIP**

Instead of Lancashire cheese, you could sprinkle Cotswold cheese over the top. This is a tasty blend of Double Gloucester, onion and chives. Alternatively, you could use a mixture of cheeses, depending on what you have available.

This cooking method makes the chicken aromatic and succulent, and reduces the oil needed as the chicken and vegetables cook in their own juices.

Italian Chicken Parcels

1 Cut 6 pieces of foil, each measuring about 25-cm/10-inches square. Brush the foil squares lightly with the olive oil and reserve until required.

2 Using a sharp knife, deeply slash each chicken breast 3–4 times at regular intervals. Cut the mozzarella cheese into fairly thin slices and tuck the slices neatly between the slashes in each of the chicken breasts.

3 Divide the courgettes and tomatoes between the pieces of foil and season to taste with pepper. Tear or roughly chop the basil or oregano and scatter over the vegetables in each parcel.

4 Place the chicken on top of each pile of vegetables, then wrap in the foil, tucking in the ends.

5 Place on a baking tray and bake in a preheated oven, 200°C/400°C/Gas Mark 6, for about 30 minutes.

6 To serve, unwrap each foil parcel and serve with freshly cooked rice or pasta.

SERVES 4

1 tbsp olive oil
6 skinless chicken breast fillets
250 g/9 oz mozzarella cheese
500 g/1 lb 2 oz courgettes, sliced
6 large tomatoes, sliced
1 small bunch of fresh basil or oregano
pepper
freshly cooked rice or pasta, to serve

NUTRITION
Calories *234*; Sugars *5 g*; Protein *28 g*;
Carbohydrate *5 g*; Fat *12 g*; Saturates *5 g*

easy

25 mins

30 mins

🍴 **COOK'S TIP**

To aid cooking, place the vegetables and chicken on the shiny side of the foil so that once the parcel is wrapped the dull surface of the foil is facing outwards. This ensures that the heat is absorbed into the parcel.

Chicken breasts are stuffed with ricotta, nutmeg and spinach, then wrapped with wafer-thin slices of Parma ham and cooked in white wine.

Parma-wrapped Chicken

SERVES 4

125 g/4½ oz frozen spinach, thawed
125 g/4½ oz ricotta cheese
pinch of freshly grated nutmeg
4 skinless, boneless chicken breasts,
   about 175 g/6 oz each
4 slices Parma ham
2 tbsp butter
1 tbsp olive oil
12 small onions or shallots
125 g/4½ oz button mushrooms, sliced
1 tbsp plain flour
150 ml/5 fl oz dry white or red wine
300 ml/10 fl oz chicken stock
salt and pepper

to serve
carrot purée
freshly cooked French beans

1 Place the spinach in a sieve and press out the water with a spoon. Mix with the ricotta and nutmeg and season to taste with salt and pepper.

2 Using a sharp knife, slit each chicken breast through the side and enlarge each cut to form a pocket. Fill with the spinach mixture, reshape the chicken breasts, wrap each breast tightly in a slice of ham and secure with cocktail sticks. Cover and leave to chill in the refrigerator.

3 Heat the butter and olive oil in a heavy-based frying pan over a low heat. Add the chicken breasts and brown for 2 minutes on each side, then transfer to a large, shallow ovenproof dish and keep warm until required.

4 Add the onions and mushrooms to the frying pan and fry over a medium heat, stirring occasionally, for 2–3 minutes until lightly browned. Stir in the flour, then gradually stir in the wine and stock. Bring to the boil, stirring constantly and cook until thickened. Season to taste with salt and pepper. Spoon the mixture around the chicken.

5 Cook the chicken, uncovered, in a preheated oven, 200°C/400°F/Gas Mark 6, for about 20 minutes. Turn the chicken breasts over and cook for a further 10 minutes. Remove the cocktail sticks and serve the chicken with the sauce, together with carrot purée and freshly cooked French beans.

NUTRITION
Calories *426*; Sugars *4 g*; Protein *44 g*;
Carbohydrate *9 g*; Fat *21 g*; Saturates *8 g*

moderate

30 mins

45 mins

These little foil parcels retain all the natural juices of the chicken making a superb sauce for the pasta.

Italian Chicken Spirals

1 Beat the chicken breasts with a rolling pin to flatten evenly.

2 Place the basil and hazelnuts in a food processor and process until finely chopped. Mix with the garlic and salt and pepper to taste.

3 Spread the basil mixture over the chicken breasts and roll up from a short end to enclose the filling. Wrap the chicken rolls tightly in foil so that they hold their shape, then seal the ends well. Place the rolls on a baking tray and bake in a preheated oven, 200°C/400°F/Gas Mark 6, for 20–25 minutes.

4 Meanwhile, bring a large saucepan of lightly salted water to the boil over a medium heat. Add the fusilli, bring back to the boil and cook for about 8–10 minutes or until tender, but still firm to the bite.

5 Drain the pasta and return to the pan with the lemon juice, olive oil, tomatoes, capers and olives. Heat through and transfer to a warmed serving dish.

6 Check that the chicken is cooked through by piercing the rolls with a skewer to make sure that the juices run clear. Slice the chicken and arrange the slices over the pasta in the serving dish. Serve immediately.

 COOK'S TIP

Sun-dried tomatoes have a wonderful, rich flavour, but if they're unavailable, use fresh tomatoes instead.

SERVES 4

4 skinless, boneless chicken breasts
25 g/1 oz fresh basil leaves
15 g/½ oz hazelnuts
1 garlic clove, crushed
250 g/9 oz dried wholemeal fusilli
1 tbsp lemon juice
1 tbsp olive oil
2 sun-dried tomatoes in oil, drained or fresh tomatoes, diced
1 tbsp capers, rinsed
55 g/2 oz stoned black olives
salt and pepper

NUTRITION
Calories 367; Sugars 1 g; Protein 33 g; Carbohydrate 35 g; Fat 12 g; Saturates 2 g

★★★ moderate
20 mins
40 mins

Chicken pieces are cooked in a succulent, mild mustard sauce, then coated in poppy seeds and served on a bed of fresh pasta shells.

Mustard Baked Chicken

SERVES 4

4 large or 8 small chicken pieces
4 tbsp butter, melted
4 tbsp mild mustard (see Cook's Tip)
2 tbsp lemon juice
1 tbsp brown sugar
1 tsp paprika
3 tbsp poppy seeds
400 g/14 oz dried pasta shells
1 tbsp olive oil
salt and pepper
cracked black pepper, to garnish

1 Arrange the chicken pieces in a single layer in a large ovenproof dish.

2 Mix the butter, mustard, lemon juice, sugar and paprika together in a bowl and season to taste with salt and pepper. Brush half the mixture over the upper surfaces of the chicken pieces and bake in a preheated oven, 200°C/400°F/Gas Mark 6, for 15 minutes.

3 Remove the dish from the oven and carefully turn the chicken pieces over, using tongs. Coat the upper surfaces of the chicken with the remaining mustard mixture, sprinkle the chicken pieces with the poppy seeds and return to the oven for a further 15 minutes.

4 Meanwhile, bring a large saucepan of lightly salted water to the boil over a medium heat. Add the pasta shells and olive oil, bring back to the boil and cook for 8–10 minutes or until tender, but still firm to the bite.

5 Drain the pasta thoroughly and divide between 4 warmed serving plates. Top the pasta with 1 or 2 of the chicken pieces, pour over the sauce and garnish with cracked pepper. Serve immediately.

NUTRITION
Calories 652; Sugars 5 g; Protein 51 g;
Carbohydrate 46 g; Fat 31 g; Saturates 12 g

easy

10 mins

35 mins

COOK'S TIP

Dijon is the type of mustard most often used in cooking, as it has a clean and only mildly spicy flavour. German mustard has a sweet-sour taste, with Bavarian mustard being slightly sweeter. American mustard is mild and sweet.

Tender lean chicken is baked with pasta in a creamy low-fat sauce, which contrasts well with the fennel and the sweetness of the raisins.

Chicken Pasta Bake

1 Trim the fennel, reserving the green fronds, and slice the bulbs thinly.

2 Toss the onions in the lemon juice and quarter the mushrooms.

3 Heat the olive oil in a large frying pan over a medium heat. Add the fennel, onion and mushrooms and fry for 4–5 minutes, stirring constantly, until just softened. Season well with salt and pepper and transfer the mixture to a large bowl. Reserve.

4 Bring a large saucepan of lightly salted water to the boil over a medium heat. Add the penne, bring back to the boil and cook for 8–10 minutes or until tender, but still firm to the bite. Drain and mix with the vegetables.

5 Stir the raisins and chicken into the pasta mixture. Beat the soft cheese to soften it, then mix into the pasta and chicken – the heat from the pasta should make the cheese melt slightly.

6 Put the mixture into a large ovenproof dish and place on a baking tray. Arrange slices of mozzarella cheese over the top and sprinkle with the grated Parmesan cheese.

7 Bake in a preheated oven, 200°C/400°F/Gas Mark 6, for 20–25 minutes until golden-brown and the top is bubbling.

8 Garnish with the reserved chopped fennel fronds and serve hot.

SERVES 4

2 fennel bulbs
2 red onions, sliced very thinly
1 tbsp lemon juice
125 g/4½ oz button mushrooms
1 tbsp olive oil
225 g/8 oz dried penne
55 g/2 oz raisins
225 g/8 oz lean, boneless cooked chicken, skinned and shredded
375 g/13 oz low-fat soft cheese with garlic and herbs
125 g/4½ oz low-fat mozzarella cheese, sliced thinly
35 g/1¼ oz freshly grated Parmesan cheese
salt and pepper

NUTRITION
Calories 380; Sugars 15 g; Protein 39 g;
Carbohydrate 27 g; Fat 14 g; Saturates 6 g

 challenging
15 mins
45 mins

You can use your favourite mushrooms, such as chanterelles or oyster mushrooms, for this delicately flavoured dish.

Chicken *and* Ham Lasagne

S E R V E S 4

1 tbsp butter, for greasing
14 sheets precooked lasagne
850 ml/1½ pints Béchamel Sauce
   (see page 73)
85 g/3 oz freshly grated Parmesan cheese

sauce
2 tbsp olive oil
2 garlic cloves, crushed
1 large onion, chopped finely
225 g/8 oz wild mushrooms, sliced
300 g/10½ oz fresh chicken mince
85 g/3 oz chicken livers, chopped finely
115 g/4 oz Parma ham, diced
150 ml/5 fl oz Marsala wine
280 g/10 oz canned chopped tomatoes
1 tbsp chopped fresh basil leaves
2 tbsp tomato purée
salt and pepper

N U T R I T I O N
Calories 708; Sugars 17 g; Protein 35 g;
Carbohydrate 57 g; Fat 35 g; Saturates 14 g

challenging

40 mins

1 hr 45 mins

1 To make the sauce, heat the olive oil in a large saucepan over a low heat. Add the garlic, onion and wild mushrooms and cook, stirring frequently, for 6 minutes.

2 Add the chicken mince, chicken livers and Parma ham and cook, stirring frequently, for about 12 minutes or until the meat has browned.

3 Stir the Marsala wine, tomatoes, basil and tomato purée into the mixture in the saucepan and cook for 4 minutes. Season to taste with salt and pepper, cover and simmer gently for 30 minutes. Uncover the pan, stir thoroughly and simmer for a further 15 minutes.

4 Lightly grease an ovenproof dish with the butter. Arrange sheets of lasagne over the base of the dish, spoon over a layer of the sauce, then spoon over a layer of béchamel sauce. Place another layer of lasagne on top and repeat the process twice, finishing with a layer of béchamel sauce. Sprinkle over the Parmesan cheese and bake in a preheated oven, 190°C/375°F/Gas Mark 5, for 35 minutes until golden-brown and bubbling. Serve immediately.

This impressive looking turkey loaf is flavoured with herbs and a layer of juicy tomatoes and covered with courgette ribbons.

Turkey *and* Vegetable Loaf

1 Line a 900-g/2-lb non-stick loaf tin with baking paper. Place the onion, garlic and turkey in a bowl, add the fresh herbs and season to taste with salt and pepper. Mix together with your hands, then add the egg white to bind.

2 Press half of the turkey mixture into the base of the prepared tin. Thinly slice the medium courgette and the tomatoes and arrange the slices over the meat. Top with the rest of the turkey mixture and press down firmly.

3 Cover with foil and place in a large roasting tin. Pour in enough boiling water to come halfway up the sides of the loaf tin. Bake in a preheated oven, 190°C/375°F/Gas Mark 5, for about 1–1¼ hours, removing the foil for the last 20 minutes of cooking. Test that the loaf is cooked by inserting a skewer into the centre – the juices should run clear. The loaf will also shrink away from the sides of the tin.

4 Meanwhile, trim the large courgette. Using a vegetable peeler or hand-held metal cheese slicer, cut the courgette lengthways into thin slices. Bring a small saucepan of water to the boil over a medium heat. Add the courgette ribbons and blanch for 1–2 minutes until just tender. Drain and keep warm.

5 Remove the turkey loaf from the tin and transfer to a warmed serving plate. Drape the courgette ribbons over the turkey loaf, garnish with mixed fresh herbs and serve immediately.

SERVES 6

1 onion, chopped finely
1 garlic clove, crushed
900 g/2 lb fresh turkey mince
1 tbsp chopped fresh parsley
1 tbsp snipped fresh chives
1 tbsp chopped fresh tarragon
1 egg white, beaten lightly
2 courgettes, 1 medium, 1 large
2 tomatoes
salt and pepper
mixed fresh herbs, to garnish

NUTRITION
Calories *165*; Sugars *1 g*; Protein *36 g*;
Carbohydrate *1 g*; Fat *2 g*; Saturates *0.5 g*

⭐⭐ easy

🟢 10 mins

 1 hr 15 mins

BAKING

The richness of the duck meat contrasts well with the apricot sauce. If duck portions are unavailable, use a whole bird cut into even-sized joints.

Roast Duck *with* Apple

SERVES 4

4 duck portions, about 350 g/12 oz each
4 tbsp dark soy sauce
2 tbsp light muscovado sugar
2 red-skinned apples
2 green-skinned apples
juice of 1 lemon
2 tbsp clear honey
a few bay leaves
salt and pepper
assorted fresh vegetables, to serve

sauce
400 g/14 oz canned apricots in fruit juice
4 tbsp sweet sherry

1 Wash the duck and trim away any excess fat. Place on a wire rack over a roasting tin and prick all over with a fork or a clean, sharp needle.

2 Brush the duck with the soy sauce. Sprinkle over the sugar and season to taste with pepper. Cook in a preheated oven, 190°C/375°F/Gas Mark 5, basting occasionally, for 50–60 minutes or until the meat is cooked through – the juices should run clear when a skewer is inserted into the thickest part of the meat.

3 Meanwhile, core the apples and cut each into 6 wedges. Place in a small roasting tin and mix with the lemon juice and honey. Add a few bay leaves and season to taste with salt and pepper. Cook alongside the duck, basting occasionally, for 20–25 minutes until tender. Discard the bay leaves.

4 To make the sauce, place the apricots in a blender or food processor with the can juices and sherry and process until smooth. Alternatively, mash the apricots with a fork until smooth and mix with the juices and sherry.

5 Just before serving, heat the apricot sauce in a small saucepan. Remove the skin from the duck and pat the flesh with kitchen paper to absorb any fat. Serve the duck with the apple wedges, apricot sauce and fresh vegetables.

NUTRITION
Calories 316; Sugars 38 g; Protein 25 g; Carbohydrate 40 g; Fat 6 g; Saturates 1 g

⊛ COOK'S TIP

Fruit complements duck perfectly. Use canned pineapple in natural juice for a delicious alternative.

moderate

10 mins

1 hr 30 mins

Chinese-style duck is very easy to prepare and makes an impressive main course for a dinner party whatever the occasion.

Honey-glazed Duck

1 Mix the soy sauce, honey, vinegar, garlic and star anise together. Blend the cornflour with the water to form a smooth paste and stir it into the mixture.

2 Place the duck breasts in a large, shallow ovenproof dish. Brush with the soy marinade, turning them to coat completely. Cover and leave to marinate in the refrigerator for at least 2 hours or overnight.

3 Remove the duck from the marinade and cook in a preheated oven, 220°C/425°F/Gas Mark 7, for 20–25 minutes, basting frequently with the glaze.

4 Remove the duck from the oven and arrange on a grill rack. Cook under a preheated hot grill for 3–4 minutes to caramelize the top, without charring.

5 Remove the duck from the grill pan and cut it into thin slices. Arrange the duck slices on a warmed serving dish, garnish with celery leaves, cucumber wedges and chives and serve immediately.

SERVES 4

1 tsp dark soy sauce
2 tbsp clear honey
1 tsp white wine vinegar
3 garlic cloves, crushed
1 tsp ground star anise
2 tsp cornflour
2 tsp water
2 large boneless duckling breasts, about 225 g/8 oz each

to garnish
celery leaves
cucumber wedges
handful of fresh chives

NUTRITION
Calories *230*; Sugars *9 g*; Protein *23 g*; Carbohydrate *14 g*; Fat *9 g*; Saturates *3 g*

  easy

2 hrs 45 mins

30 mins

COOK'S TIP

If the duck begins to burn slightly while it is cooking in the oven, cover with foil. Check that the duck breasts are cooked through by inserting the point of a sharp knife into the thickest part of the flesh – the juices should run clear.

In this traditional Chinese dish the pork turns 'red' during cooking because it is basted in dark soy sauce.

Red Roast Pork *in* Soy Sauce

SERVES 4

450 g/1 lb lean pork fillets
6 tbsp dark soy sauce
2 tbsp dry sherry
1 tsp Chinese five-spice powder
2 garlic cloves, crushed
2 tsp finely chopped fresh root ginger
1 large red pepper
1 large yellow pepper
1 large orange pepper
4 tbsp caster sugar
2 tbsp red wine vinegar

to garnish
spring onions, shredded
handful of fresh chives

NUTRITION
Calories *268*; Sugars *20 g*; Protein *26 g*;
Carbohydrate *22 g*; Fat *8 g*; Saturates *3 g*

 moderate
 1 hr 15 mins
1 hr 15 mins

1 Trim away any excess fat and silver skin from the pork and place in a large, shallow dish.

2 Mix the soy sauce, sherry, Chinese five-spice powder, garlic and ginger together in a bowl. Spoon the mixture over the pork, turning it to coat, cover and leave to marinate in the refrigerator for at least 1 hour or until required.

3 Drain the pork, reserving the marinade. Place the pork on a roasting rack over a roasting tin. Cook in a preheated oven, 190°C/375°F/Gas Mark 5, basting occasionally with the marinade, for 1 hour or until cooked through.

5 Meanwhile, halve and deseed the red, yellow and orange peppers. Cut each pepper half into 3 equal pieces. Arrange them on a baking tray and bake alongside the pork for the last 30 minutes of the cooking time.

6 Place the sugar and vinegar in a saucepan and heat gently until the sugar dissolves. Bring to the boil and simmer for 3–4 minutes until syrupy.

7 When the pork is cooked, remove it from the oven and brush with the sugar syrup. Leave for about 5 minutes, then slice and arrange on a serving platter with the peppers, garnished with the spring onions and chives. Serve.

Cannelloni, the thick, round pasta tubes, make perfect containers for close-textured fillings of all kinds.

Stuffed Cannelloni

1 To make the filling, melt the butter in a saucepan over a low heat. Add the spinach and stir-fry for 2–3 minutes. Remove from the heat and stir in the ricotta and Parmesan cheeses and the ham. Season to taste with nutmeg, salt and pepper. Beat in the cream and eggs to make a thick paste.

2 Bring a large saucepan of lightly salted water to the boil over a medium heat. Add the cannelloni tubes and olive oil, bring back to the boil and cook for 10–12 minutes or until almost tender. Drain and leave to cool.

3 To make the sauce, melt the butter in a pan over a low heat. Stir in the flour and cook, stirring, for 1 minute. Gradually stir in the milk. Add the bay leaves and simmer, stirring, for 5 minutes. Add the nutmeg and salt and pepper to taste. Remove from the heat and discard the bay leaves.

4 Spoon the filling into a piping bag and fill the cannelloni tubes.

5 Spoon a little sauce into the base of an ovenproof dish. Place the cannelloni in a single layer in the dish and pour over the remaining sauce. Sprinkle over the Parmesan cheese and bake in a preheated oven, 190°C/375°F/Gas Mark 5, for 40–45 minutes. Garnish with fresh herb sprigs and serve.

COOK'S TIP

If you prefer, use fresh spinach instead of frozen, but make sure the quantity of fresh spinach is doubled.

SERVES 4

8 dried cannelloni tubes
1 tbsp olive oil
25 g/1 oz freshly grated Parmesan cheese
fresh herb sprigs, to garnish

filling

2 tbsp butter
300 g/10½ oz frozen spinach, thawed and chopped
115 g/4 oz ricotta cheese
25 g/1 oz freshly grated Parmesan cheese
55 g/2 oz chopped ham
pinch of freshly grated nutmeg
2 tbsp double cream
2 eggs, beaten lightly
salt and pepper

béchamel sauce

2 tbsp butter
2½ tbsp plain flour
300 ml/10 fl oz milk
2 bay leaves
pinch of freshly grated nutmeg

NUTRITION

Calories *520*; Sugars *5 g*; Protein *21 g*; Carbohydrate *23 g*; Fat *39 g*; Saturates *18 g*

 moderate

 30 mins

1 hr 15 mins

This unusual recipe uses chicken and Cumberland sausage, which can then be made into individual bite-sized cakes.

Tom's Toad-in-the-Hole

SERVES 4 – 6

125 g/4½ oz plain flour
pinch of salt
1 egg, beaten
200 ml/7 fl oz milk
5 tbsp water
2 tbsp beef dripping or oil
250 g/9 oz chicken breasts
250 g/9 oz Cumberland sausage

to serve
chicken or onion gravy, optional
creamy mashed potato

1 Mix the flour and salt together in a bowl. Make a well in the centre and add the beaten egg.

2 Add half of the milk and, using a wooden spoon, work in the flour slowly. Beat the mixture until smooth, then add the remaining milk and water. Beat again until the mixture is smooth. Leave to stand for at least 1 hour.

3 Add the dripping or oil to individual Yorkshire pudding tins or to 1 large roasting tin. Cut up the chicken and sausage so that you get a generous piece in each individual tin or several scattered around the large tin.

4 Heat the tins or tin in a preheated oven, 220°C/425°F/Gas Mark 7, for about 5 minutes until very hot. Remove the tins from the oven and pour in the batter, leaving space for the mixture to expand.

5 Return to the oven to cook for about 35–45 minutes until risen and golden-brown. Do not open the oven door for at least 30 minutes.

6 Serve the toad-in-the-hole piping hot with chicken or onion gravy and creamy mashed potato.

NUTRITION
Calories *470*; Sugars *4 g*; Protein *28 g*;
Carbohydrate *30 g*; Fat *27 g*; Saturates *12 g*

easy

1 hr 15 mins

40–50 mins

COOK'S TIP

Use skinless, boneless chicken legs instead of chicken breast in the recipe and cut up as directed. Instead of Cumberland sausage, use your favourite variety of sausage.

A hot pot is a lamb casserole made with carrots and onions and with a potato topping. The steaks used here are an interesting alternative.

Hot Pot Steaks

1 Using a small, sharp knife, trim any excess fat from the lamb steaks.

2 Season both sides of the steaks with salt and pepper to taste and arrange them in a single layer on a baking tray.

3 Alternate layers of sliced onion, carrot and potato on top of each lamb steak, ending with a layer of potato.

4 Brush the tops of the potato lightly with olive oil, season well with salt and pepper, then sprinkle with a little dried rosemary.

5 Bake in a preheated oven, 180°C/350°F/Gas Mark 4, for 25–30 minutes or until the lamb is tender and cooked through.

6 Drain the lamb on kitchen paper and transfer to a warmed serving plate.

7 Garnish with fresh rosemary sprigs and serve accompanied with a selection of steamed green vegetables.

SERVES 4

4 lean, boneless lamb leg steaks,
    about 125 g/4½ oz each
1 small onion, sliced thinly
1 carrot, sliced thinly
1 potato, sliced thinly
1 tsp olive oil
1 tsp dried rosemary
salt and pepper
fresh rosemary sprigs, to garnish
freshly steamed green vegetables, to serve

NUTRITION
Calories 250; Sugars 2 g; Protein 27 g;
Carbohydrate 8 g; Fat 12 g; Saturates 5 g

      easy

      10 mins

      30 mins

🧑‍🍳 **COOK'S TIP**

This recipe would work equally well with boneless chicken breasts. Pound the chicken slightly with a meat mallet or covered rolling pin so the pieces are the same thickness throughout.

A satisfying bake of lean minced beef, courgettes and tomatoes cooked in a low-fat 'custard' with a cheesy crust.

Beef *and* Tomato Gratin

SERVES 4

350 g/12 oz lean beef mince
1 large onion, chopped finely
1 tsp dried mixed herbs
1 tbsp plain flour
300 ml/10 fl oz beef stock
1 tbsp tomato purée
2 large tomatoes, sliced thinly
4 courgettes, sliced thinly
2 tbsp cornflour
300 ml/10 fl oz skimmed milk
150 ml/5 fl oz low-fat fromage frais
1 egg yolk
70 g/2½ oz freshly grated Parmesan cheese
salt and pepper

1 Dry-fry the beef and onion in a large, heavy-based frying pan over a low heat, stirring frequently, for 4–5 minutes until the meat is browned.

2 Stir in the dried mixed herbs, flour, stock and tomato purée and season to taste with salt and pepper. Bring to the boil, reduce the heat and simmer gently for 30 minutes or until the mixture has thickened.

3 Transfer the beef mixture to an ovenproof gratin dish. Cover with a layer of the sliced tomatoes and then add a layer of sliced courgettes.

4 Blend the cornflour with a little milk to make a smooth paste. Pour the remaining milk into a saucepan and bring to the boil over a low heat. Add the cornflour mixture and cook, stirring constantly, for 1–2 minutes until thickened. Remove from the heat and beat in the fromage frais and egg yolk. Season to taste with salt and pepper.

5 Spread the white sauce over the layer of courgettes. Place the dish on a baking sheet and sprinkle with the Parmesan cheese. Bake in a preheated oven, 190°C/375°F/Gas Mark 5, for about 25–30 minutes or until the topping is golden-brown and bubbling. Serve hot.

NUTRITION
Calories *278*; Sugars *10 g*; Protein *29 g*;
Carbohydrate *20 g*; Fat *10 g*; Saturates *4 g*

⭐⭐⭐ moderate

 10 mins

 1 hr 15 mins

🧑‍🍳 **COOK'S TIP**

Try replacing the beef mince with lamb and the courgettes with aubergines for an easy Moussaka.

This slow-cooked beef stew is flavoured with an aromatic mixture of oranges, red wine and porcini mushrooms.

Rich Beef Stew

1 Heat the vegetable oil and butter in a large frying pan over a low heat. Add the onions and fry, stirring occasionally, for about 5 minutes or until golden. Remove the onions with a slotted spoon, and keep warm.

2 Add the beef to the frying pan and cook, stirring constantly, for 5 minutes or until browned all over.

3 Return the onions to the frying pan and add the stock, wine, oregano and sugar, stirring to mix well. Transfer the mixture to a casserole dish.

4 Pare the rind from the orange and cut it into strips. Slice the orange flesh into rings. Add the orange rings and the rind to the casserole and cook in a preheated oven, 180°C/350°F/Gas Mark 4, for 1¼ hours.

5 Meanwhile, soak the porcini mushrooms in 4 tablespoons of warm water for 30 minutes.

6 Peel and halve the tomatoes. Add the tomatoes, porcini mushrooms and their soaking liquid to the casserole. Cook for a further 20 minutes until the beef is tender and the juices thickened. Serve with cooked rice or potatoes.

COOK'S TIP

If you cannot find dried porcini mushrooms, use sliced fresh mushrooms instead, and omit Step 5.

SERVES 4

1 tbsp vegetable oil
1 tbsp butter
225 g/8 oz baby onions, peeled and halved
600 g/1 lb 5 oz stewing steak,
    diced into 4-cm/1½-inch cubes
300 ml/10 fl oz beef stock
150 ml/5 fl oz red wine
4 tbsp chopped fresh oregano
1 tbsp sugar
1 orange
25 g/1 oz dried porcini mushrooms
225 g/8 oz fresh plum tomatoes
freshly cooked rice or potatoes, to serve

NUTRITION
Calories *388*; Sugars *15 g*; Protein *30 g*;
Carbohydrate *16 g*; Fat *21 g*; Saturates *9 g*

  moderate

45 mins

  1 hr 45 mins

A different twist is given to this traditional and ever-popular pasta dish with a rich, but subtle sauce.

Meatballs *in* Red Wine Sauce

SERVES 4

150 ml/5 fl oz milk
150 g/5½ oz fresh white breadcrumbs
2 tbsp butter
9 tbsp olive oil
225 g/8 oz sliced oyster mushrooms
2½ tbsp wholemeal flour
200 ml/7 fl oz beef stock
150 ml/5 fl oz red wine
4 tomatoes, peeled and chopped
1 tbsp tomato purée
1 tsp brown sugar
1 tbsp finely chopped fresh basil
12 shallots, chopped
450 g/1 lb beef steak mince
1 tsp paprika
450 g/1 lb dried tagliatelle
salt and pepper
fresh basil sprigs, to garnish

NUTRITION

Calories *811*; Sugars *7 g*; Protein *30 g*;
Carbohydrate *76 g*; Fat *43 g*; Saturates *12 g*

moderate

45 mins

1 hr 30 mins

1 Pour the milk into a small bowl, add the breadcrumbs and leave to soak for 30 minutes.

2 Heat half of the butter and 4 tablespoons of the olive oil in a saucepan over a low heat. Add the mushrooms and fry for 4 minutes, then stir in the flour and cook for 2 minutes. Add the stock and wine and simmer for 15 minutes. Add the tomatoes, tomato purée, sugar and basil. Season to taste with salt and pepper and simmer for 30 minutes.

3 Mix the shallots, steak and paprika with the soaked breadcrumbs and season to taste with salt and pepper. Shape the mixture into 14 meatballs.

4 Heat 4 tablespoons of the remaining olive oil and butter in a large frying pan over a medium heat. Add the meatballs and fry, turning frequently, until browned all over. Transfer to a deep casserole, pour over the red wine sauce, cover and bake in a preheated oven, 180°C/350°F/Gas Mark 4, for 30 minutes.

5 Bring a large saucepan of lightly salted water to the boil over a medium heat. Add the tagliatelle and the remaining olive oil, bring back to the boil and cook for 8–10 minutes or until tender, but still firm to the bite. Drain and transfer to a serving dish. Remove the casserole from the oven and leave to cool for 3 minutes. Pour the meatballs and sauce on to the pasta, garnish with a few sprigs of fresh basil and serve.

Any variety of long pasta, such as tagliatelle or fettuccine, could be used for this very tasty dish from Sicily.

Sicilian Spaghetti Cake

1 Brush a 20-cm/8-inch loose-bottomed round cake tin with olive oil and line the base with oiled baking paper. Cut the aubergines into slanting slices 5-mm/¼-inch thick. Heat some of the olive oil in a frying pan over a low heat. Add a few slices of aubergine at a time and fry until lightly browned, turning once, and adding more oil as necessary. Drain on kitchen paper.

2 Put the minced beef, onion and garlic into a saucepan and dry-fry over a low heat, stirring frequently, until browned all over. Add the tomato purée, tomatoes, Worcestershire sauce and herbs and season to taste with salt and pepper. Simmer gently for 10 minutes, stirring occasionally, then add the olives and pepper and cook for a further 10 minutes.

3 Bring a large saucepan of lightly salted water to the boil over a medium heat. Add the spaghetti, bring back to the boil and cook for 8–10 minutes or until tender, but still firm to the bite. Drain and transfer to a bowl. Mix in the meat mixture and Parmesan cheese, tossing together with 2 forks.

4 Lay overlapping slices of aubergine over the base and up the sides of the prepared cake tin. Add the meat mixture and cover with the remaining aubergine slices.

5 Stand the cake tin in a roasting tin and cook in a preheated oven, 200°C/400°F/Gas Mark 6, for 40 minutes. Remove from the oven, leave to stand in the tin for 5 minutes, then loosen around the edges and invert on to a warmed serving dish, releasing the tin clip. Remove and discard the baking paper. Serve immediately.

S E R V E S   4

150 ml/5 fl oz olive oil, plus extra for brushing
2 aubergines
350 g/12 oz finely minced lean beef
1 onion, chopped
2 garlic cloves, crushed
2 tbsp tomato purée
400 g/14 oz canned chopped tomatoes
1 tsp Worcestershire sauce
1 tsp chopped fresh oregano or marjoram or ½ tsp dried oregano or marjoram
40 g/1½ oz stoned black olives, sliced
1 green, red or yellow pepper, deseeded and chopped
175 g/6 oz dried spaghetti
125 g/4½ oz freshly grated Parmesan cheese
salt and pepper

N U T R I T I O N
Calories 876; Sugars 10 g; Protein 37 g; Carbohydrate 39 g; Fat 65 g; Saturates 18 g

moderate

30 mins

1 hr 20 mins

The sauce in this delicious baked pasta dish can also be used as an alternative sauce for the classic Spaghetti Bolognese.

Lasagne Verde

SERVES 6

Ragù Sauce (see page 15)
1 tbsp olive oil
225 g/8 oz fresh or dried lasagne verde
1 tbsp butter, for greasing
850 ml/1½ pints Béchamel Sauce
   (see page 73)
55 g/2oz freshly grated Parmesan cheese
salt and pepper
mixed salad leaves, to serve

NUTRITION
Calories *619*; Sugars *7 g*; Protein *29 g*;
Carbohydrate *21 g*; Fat *45 g*; Saturates *19 g*

⭐⭐⭐⭐ challenging
🟢 1 hr 45 mins
🔵 1 hr

1 Make the ragù sauce, but cook for 10–12 minutes longer than the time given, in an uncovered saucepan, to allow the excess liquid to evaporate. It needs to be reduced to the consistency of a thick paste.

2 Have ready a large saucepan of lightly salted boiling water and add the olive oil. Drop the lasagne sheets into the boiling water, a few at a time, and bring the water back to the boil before adding further lasagne sheets. If you are using fresh lasagne, cook the sheets for a total of 8 minutes. If you are using dried pasta or partly precooked pasta, cook it according to the instructions given on the packet.

3 Remove the pasta sheets from the saucepan with a slotted spoon. Spread them out in a single layer on clean, damp tea towels.

4 Grease a rectangular ovenproof dish, about 25–28-cm/10–11-inches long with the butter. To assemble the dish, spoon a little of the meat sauce into the prepared dish, cover with a layer of lasagne, then spoon over a little béchamel sauce and sprinkle with some of the Parmesan cheese. Continue making layers in this way, covering the final layer of lasagne sheets with the remaining béchamel sauce.

5 Sprinkle the remaining Parmesan cheese over the top and bake in a preheated oven, 190°C/375°F/Gas Mark 5, for 40 minutes or until the sauce is golden-brown and bubbling. Serve with mixed salad leaves.

A recipe that has both Italian and Greek origins, this dish may be served hot or cold, cut into thick, satisfying squares.

Pasticcio

1 To make the sauce, heat the olive oil in a large frying pan over a medium heat. Add the onion and red pepper and fry for 3 minutes. Stir in the garlic and cook for 1 further minute. Stir in the beef and cook, stirring frequently, until completely sealed.

2 Add the chopped tomatoes and wine, stir well and bring to the boil. Simmer, uncovered, for 20 minutes or until the sauce is fairly thick. Stir in the parsley and anchovies and season to taste with salt and pepper.

3 Bring a large saucepan of lightly salted water to the boil over a medium heat. Add the fusilli and olive oil, bring back to the boil and cook for 8–10 minutes or until tender, but still firm to the bite. Drain, then transfer the fusilli to a bowl. Stir in the cream and reserve.

4 To make the topping, beat the yogurt, eggs and nutmeg together until well combined and season to taste with salt and pepper.

5 Brush a large, shallow ovenproof dish with olive oil. Spoon in half of the pasta mixture and cover with half of the meat sauce. Repeat these layers, then spread the topping evenly over the final layer. Sprinkle the Parmesan cheese evenly on top.

6 Bake in a preheated oven, 190°C/375°F/Gas Mark 5, for 25 minutes or until the topping is golden-brown and bubbling. Garnish with a few sprigs of fresh rosemary and serve immediately.

SERVES 6

225 g/8 oz dried fusilli, or other short pasta shapes
1 tbsp olive oil, plus extra for brushing
4 tbsp double cream
fresh rosemary sprigs, to garnish

sauce

2 tbsp olive oil
1 onion, sliced thinly
1 red pepper, deseeded and chopped
2 garlic cloves, chopped
625 g/1 lb 6 oz lean beef mince
400 g/14 oz canned chopped tomatoes
125 ml/4 fl oz dry white wine
2 tbsp chopped fresh parsley
50 g/1¾ oz canned anchovies, drained and chopped
salt and pepper

topping

300 ml/10 fl oz natural yogurt
3 eggs
pinch of freshly grated nutmeg
40 g/1½ oz freshly grated Parmesan cheese

NUTRITION
Calories 590; Sugars 8 g; Protein 34 g; Carbohydrate 23 g; Fat 39 g; Saturates 16 g

 moderate

35 mins

1 hr 15 mins

Vegan *and* Vegetarian

Anyone who ever thought that vegetarian meals were dull will be proved wrong by the rich variety of dishes in this chapter. You'll recognise influences from Middle Eastern and Italian cooking, such as the Pasta and Bean Casserole, Roman Focaccia, and Sun-dried Tomato Loaf, but there are also traditional recipes such as Baked Cheesecake and Fruit Crumble. They all make exciting treats at any time of year and for virtually any occasion. Don't be afraid to substitute your own personal favourite ingredients wherever appropriate.

Thick pasta tubes are filled with a mixture of seasoned chopped mushrooms and baked in a rich, fragrant tomato sauce.

Mushroom Cannelloni

SERVES 4

350 g/12 oz chestnut mushrooms, chopped finely
1 onion, chopped finely
1 garlic clove, crushed
1 tbsp chopped fresh thyme
½ tsp freshly grated nutmeg
4 tbsp dry white wine
50 g/1¾ oz fresh white breadcrumbs
12 dried 'quick-cook' cannelloni tubes
salt and pepper
shavings of fresh Parmesan cheese, to garnish (optional)

tomato sauce

1 large red pepper
200 ml/7 fl oz dry white wine
450 ml/16 fl oz passata
2 tbsp tomato purée
2 bay leaves
1 tsp caster sugar

NUTRITION

Calories *156*; Sugars *8 g*; Protein *6 g*;
Carbohydrate *21 g*; Fat *1 g*; Saturates *0.2 g*

 challenging

 35 mins

🕐 1 hr 30 mins

1 Place the mushrooms, onion and garlic in a saucepan. Stir in the thyme, nutmeg and the wine. Bring to the boil over a low heat, cover and simmer for 10 minutes.

2 Stir in the breadcrumbs to bind the mixture together and season to taste with salt and pepper. Leave to cool for 10 minutes.

3 To make the sauce, halve and deseed the pepper, place on the grill rack and cook under a preheated hot grill for 8–10 minutes until charred. Leave to cool for 10 minutes.

4 Once the pepper has cooled, peel off the charred skin. Chop the flesh and place in a food processor with the wine. Blend until smooth, then pour into a pan. Mix the remaining sauce ingredients with the pepper and wine. Bring to the boil and simmer for 10 minutes. Remove and discard the bay leaves.

5 Cover the base of a large ovenproof dish with a thin layer of the sauce. Fill the cannelloni with the mushroom mixture and place in a single layer in the dish. Spoon over the remaining sauce, then cover with foil and bake in a preheated oven, 200°C/400°F/Gas Mark 6, for 35–40 minutes. Garnish with Parmesan cheese shavings, if using, and serve hot.

🍲 COOK'S TIP

Chestnut mushrooms, also known as champignons de Paris, are common cultivated mushrooms that may have brown or white caps.

A satisfying winter dish, this is a slow-cooked, one-pot meal. The haricot beans need to be soaked overnight, so prepare well in advance.

Pasta *and* Bean Casserole

1 Put the beans into a large saucepan, cover them with water and bring to the boil over a fairly high heat. Boil the beans rapidly for 20 minutes, then drain them and reserve.

2 Bring a large saucepan of lightly salted water to the boil over a medium heat. Add the penne and 1 tablespoon of the olive oil, bring back to the boil and cook for 3 minutes. Drain and reserve.

3 Place the beans in a large flameproof casserole, pour on the vegetable stock and stir in the remaining olive oil, the onions, garlic, bay leaves, herbs, wine and tomato purée.

4 Bring to the boil, cover the casserole and cook in a preheated oven, 180°C/ 350°F/Gas Mark 4, for 2 hours.

5 Remove the casserole from the oven and add the reserved pasta, the celery, fennel, mushrooms and tomatoes and season to taste with salt and pepper.

6 Stir in the sugar and sprinkle on the breadcrumbs. Cover the casserole again, return to the oven and continue cooking for 1 hour. Serve hot with mixed salad leaves.

SERVES 4

225 g/8 oz dried haricot beans, soaked overnight and drained
225 g/8 oz dried penne, or other short pasta shapes
6 tbsp olive oil
850 ml/1½ pints vegetable stock
2 large onions, sliced
2 garlic cloves, chopped
2 bay leaves
1 tsp dried oregano
1 tsp dried thyme
5 tbsp red wine
2 tbsp tomato purée
2 celery sticks, sliced
1 fennel bulb, sliced
125 g/4½ oz mushrooms, sliced
225 g/8 oz tomatoes, sliced
1 tsp dark muscovado sugar
50 g/1¾ oz dry white breadcrumbs
salt and pepper
mixed salad leaves, to serve

NUTRITION

Calories 323; Sugars 5 g; Protein 13 g; Carbohydrate 41 g; Fat 12 g; Saturates 2 g

moderate

25 mins

3 hrs 30 mins

This savoury flan combines lentils and red peppers in a tasty wholemeal pastry case. This flan is suitable for vegans.

Lentil *and* Red Pepper Flan

SERVES 6

pastry

225 g/8 oz plain wholemeal flour, plus extra for dusting
100 g/3½ oz vegan margarine, cut into small pieces
4 tbsp water

filling

175 g/6 oz split red lentils, rinsed
300 ml/10 fl oz vegetable stock
1 tbsp vegan margarine
1 onion, chopped
2 red peppers, deseeded and diced
1 tsp yeast extract
1 tbsp tomato purée
3 tbsp chopped fresh parsley
pepper

NUTRITION
Calories 374; Sugars 5 g; Protein 13 g;
Carbohydrate 44 g; Fat 17 g; Saturates 7 g

 easy

15–20 mins

50 mins

1 To make the pastry, sift the flour into a large bowl and add any bran remaining in the sieve. Add the vegan margarine and rub it in with your fingertips until the mixture resembles fine breadcrumbs. Stir in the water and bring together to form a dough. Wrap in clingfilm and leave to chill in the refrigerator for 30 minutes.

2 Meanwhile, make the filling. Put the lentils in a saucepan with the stock, bring to the boil over a medium heat, then simmer for 10 minutes until the lentils are tender and can be mashed to a purée.

3 Melt the margarine in a small pan over a low heat. Add the onion and red peppers and fry until just softened. Add the lentil purée, yeast extract, tomato purée and chopped parsley. Season to taste with pepper. Mix well.

4 Roll out the dough on a lightly floured work surface and use to line a 24-cm/9½-inch loose-bottomed quiche/flan tin. Prick the base of the pastry with a fork and spoon the lentil mixture into the pastry case.

5 Bake in a preheated oven, 200°C/400°F/Gas Mark 6, for 30 minutes until the filling is firm. Serve hot.

COOK'S TIP

Add some sweetcorn to the flan at step 4 for a colourful and tasty change, if you prefer.

A hearty casserole of black-eyed beans in a rich, sweet tomato sauce flavoured with treacle and mustard.

Spicy Black-eyed Beans

1 Rinse the beans and place in a saucepan. Cover with water, bring to the boil over a fairly high heat and boil rapidly for 10 minutes. Drain and place in a large casserole.

2 Meanwhile, heat the vegetable oil in a frying pan over a low heat. Add the onions and fry, stirring occasionally, for 5 minutes. Stir in the honey, treacle, soy sauce, mustard powder and tomato purée. Pour in the stock, bring to the boil and pour over the beans.

3 Tie the bay leaf and herbs together with a piece of string and add to the casserole. Using a vegetable peeler, pare off 3 pieces of orange rind and mix into the beans, along with plenty of pepper. Cover and cook in a preheated oven, 150°C/300°F/Gas Mark 2, for 1 hour.

4 Squeeze the juice from the orange and blend with the cornflour to form a smooth paste. Remove the casserole from the oven and stir the cornflour paste into the beans, together with the red peppers. Cover the casserole and return to the oven for 1 further hour or until the sauce is rich and thick and the beans are tender. Remove and discard the herbs and orange rind.

5 Garnish the casserole with fresh parsley and serve with crusty bread.

SERVES 4

350 g/12 oz dried black-eyed beans,
   soaked overnight in cold water
1 tbsp vegetable oil
2 onions, chopped
1 tbsp clear honey
2 tbsp treacle
4 tbsp dark soy sauce
1 tsp mustard powder
4 tbsp tomato purée
450 ml/16 fl oz vegetable stock
1 bay leaf
1 fresh rosemary sprig, thyme sprig and
   sage sprig
1 small orange
1 tbsp cornflour
2 red peppers, deseeded and diced
pepper
2 tbsp chopped fresh flat-leaf parsley,
   to garnish
crusty bread, to serve

NUTRITION

Calories 233; Sugars 21 g; Protein 11 g;
Carbohydrate 42 g; Fat 4 g; Saturates 1 g

moderate

15 mins

1 hr 30 mins

This freshly made herb bread is an ideal accompaniment to salads and soups and is suitable for vegans.

Garlic *and* Sage Bread

SERVES 6

1 tbsp vegan margarine, for greasing
250 g/9 oz strong brown bread flour, plus extra for dusting
1 sachet easy-blend dried yeast
3 tbsp chopped fresh sage
2 tsp sea salt
3 garlic cloves, chopped finely
1 tsp clear honey
150 ml/5 fl oz hand-hot water

1 Grease a baking tray with vegan margarine. Sift the flour into a large bowl and stir in the bran remaining in the sieve.

2 Stir in the dried yeast, sage and half of the sea salt. Reserve 1 teaspoon of the chopped garlic for sprinkling and stir the remainder into the bowl. Add the honey, together with the water and mix to form a dough.

3 Knead the dough on to a lightly floured work surface for about 5 minutes. Alternatively, use an electric mixer with a dough hook.

4 Place the dough in a greased bowl, cover and leave to rise in a warm place until doubled in size.

5 Knead the dough again for a few minutes, shape it into a ring (see Cook's Tip) and place on the baking tray.

6 Cover and leave to rise for a further 30 minutes or until springy to the touch. Sprinkle with the rest of the sea salt and garlic.

7 Bake in a preheated oven, 200°C/400°F/Gas Mark 6, for 25–30 minutes. Transfer the loaf to a wire rack to cool before serving.

NUTRITION
Calories 207; Sugars 3 g; Protein 9 g; Carbohydrate 42 g; Fat 2 g; Saturates 0 g

moderate

1 hr 15 mins

30 mins

COOK'S TIP

Roll the dough into a long sausage and then curve it into a circular shape. You can omit the sea salt for sprinkling, if you prefer.

Roman focaccia makes a delicious snack on its own or it can be served with soup, cheese and salad for a quick supper.

Roman Focaccia

1 Place the yeast and the sugar in a small bowl and mix with 100 ml/3½ fl oz of the water. Leave to ferment in a warm place for 15 minutes.

2 Sift the flour and salt into a large bowl. Add the yeast mixture, half of the rosemary and the remaining water and mix to form a smooth dough. Knead the dough for 4 minutes, then cover with oiled clingfilm and leave to rise for 30 minutes or until doubled in size.

3 Meanwhile, heat the olive oil in a large saucepan over a low heat. Add the onions and garlic and fry, stirring occasionally, for 5 minutes or until softened. Cover the pan and continue to cook for 7–8 minutes or until the onions are lightly caramelized.

4 Remove the dough from the bowl and knead it on a lightly floured work surface for 1–2 minutes, then roll out to form a square. The dough should be no more than 5 mm/¼ inch thick as it will rise during cooking. Place the dough on a large baking tray, pushing out the edges until even.

5 Spread the onions over the dough and sprinkle with the remaining rosemary.

6 Bake in a preheated oven, 200°C/400°F/Gas Mark 6, for 25–30 minutes or until golden-brown. Remove from the oven and leave to cool slightly. Cut the focaccia into 16 squares, garnish with a few fresh rosemary leaves and serve.

MAKES 16 SQUARES

10 g/¼ oz dried yeast
1 tsp granulated sugar
300 ml/10 fl oz hand-hot water
450 g/1 lb strong white flour, plus extra for dusting
2 tsp salt
3 tbsp chopped fresh rosemary
2 tbsp olive oil, plus extra for oiling
450 g/1 lb mixed red and white onions, sliced into rings
4 garlic cloves, sliced
fresh rosemary leaves, to garnish

NUTRITION
Calories *119*; Sugars *2 g*; Protein *3 g*;
Carbohydrate *24 g*; Fat *2 g*; Saturates *0.3 g*

✪✪✪　　moderate

🖐　　1 hr

　　45 mins

This delicious tomato bread is great with cheese or soup or for making an unusual sandwich. This recipe makes one loaf.

Sun-dried Tomato Loaf

MAKES 1 LOAF

10 g/¼ oz dried yeast
1 tsp granulated sugar
300 ml/10 fl oz hand-hot water
450 g/1 lb strong white flour, plus extra
    for dusting
1 tsp salt
2 tsp dried basil
2 tbsp sun-dried tomato paste or
    tomato purée
1 tbsp olive oil, for oiling
1 tbsp vegan margarine, for greasing
12 sun-dried tomatoes in oil, drained and
    cut into strips

NUTRITION
Calories 403; Sugars 5 g; Protein 12 g;
Carbohydrate 91 g; Fat 2 g; Saturates 0.3 g

  moderate

  1 hr 45 mins

  35 mins

1 Place the yeast and sugar in a bowl and mix with 100 ml/3½ fl oz of the water. Leave to ferment in a warm place for 15 minutes.

2 Sift the flour and salt into a bowl. Make a well in the centre and add the basil, yeast mixture, tomato paste and half of the remaining water. Using a wooden spoon, draw the flour into the liquid and mix to form a dough, adding the rest of the water a little at a time.

3 Knead the dough on a floured work surface for 5 minutes or until smooth. Cover with oiled clingfilm and leave in a warm place to rise for 30 minutes or until doubled in size.

4 Lightly grease a 900-g/2-lb loaf tin with vegan margarine.

5 Remove the dough from the bowl and knead in the sun-dried tomatoes. Knead again for 2–3 minutes.

6 Place the dough in the prepared tin and leave to rise for 30–40 minutes or until it has doubled in size again. Bake in a preheated oven, 190°C/375°F/Gas Mark 5, for 30–35 minutes or until golden and the base sounds hollow when tapped. Leave to cool on a wire rack.

COOK'S TIP

You could make mini sun-dried tomato loaves for children. Divide the dough into 8 equal portions, leave to rise and bake in mini-loaf tins for 20 minutes.

Peppers become marvellously sweet and mild when they are roasted in the oven and make this bread delicious.

Roasted Pepper Bread

1 Grease a 23-cm/9-inch deep round cake tin with vegan margarine.

2 Place the peppers and rosemary in a roasting tin. Pour over the olive oil and roast in a preheated oven, 200°C/400°F/Gas Mark 6, for 20 minutes or until charred. Remove the skin from the peppers and cut the flesh into slices.

3 Place the yeast and sugar in a small bowl and mix with 100 ml/3½ fl oz of the water. Leave to ferment in a warm place for 15 minutes.

4 Sift the flour and salt into a large bowl. Stir in the yeast mixture and the remaining water and mix to form a smooth dough.

5 Knead the dough on a floured work surface for about 5 minutes until smooth. Cover with oiled clingfilm and leave to rise for about 30 minutes or until doubled in size.

6 Cut the dough into 3 equal portions. Roll the portions into rounds slightly larger than the cake tin. Place 1 round in the base of the tin so it reaches up the sides of the tin by 2 cm/¾ inch. Top with half of the pepper mixture.

7 Place the second round of dough on top, followed by the remaining pepper mixture. Place the last round of dough on top, gently pushing the edges of the dough down the sides of the tin to enclose the peppers completely.

8 Cover the dough with oiled clingfilm and leave to rise for 30–40 minutes. Bake in the preheated oven for 45 minutes until golden or the base sounds hollow when tapped. Leave to cool slightly on a wire rack and serve warm.

SERVES 4

1 tbsp vegan margarine, for greasing
1 red pepper, halved and deseeded
1 yellow pepper, halved and deseeded
2 fresh rosemary sprigs
1 tbsp olive oil, plus extra for oiling
10 g/¼ oz dried yeast
1 tsp granulated sugar
300 ml/10 fl oz hand-hot water
450 g/1 lb strong white flour, plus extra for dusting
1 tsp salt

NUTRITION
Calories *426*; Sugars *4 g*; Protein *12 g*; Carbohydrate *90 g*; Fat *4 g*; Saturates *1 g*

★★★ moderate

 1 hr 45 mins

1 hr 5 mins

These vegan slices are ideal for children's lunches. They are full of flavour and made with lots of healthy ingredients.

Apricot Slices

MAKES 12 BARS

pastry
100 g/3½ oz vegan margarine, cut into small pieces, plus extra for greasing
225 g/8 oz wholemeal flour, plus extra for dusting
50 g/1¾ oz finely ground mixed nuts
4 tbsp water
1–2 tsp soya milk, for glazing

filling
225 g/8 oz dried apricots
grated rind of 1 orange
300 ml/10 fl oz apple juice
1 tsp ground cinnamon
50 g/1¾ oz raisins

1 Lightly grease a 23-cm/9-inch square cake tin with vegan margarine. To make the pastry, place the flour and nuts in a large bowl. Add the vegan margarine and rub in with your fingertips until the mixture resembles breadcrumbs. Stir in the water and mix to form a dough. Wrap in clingfilm and leave to chill in the refrigerator for 30 minutes.

2 To make the filling, place the apricots, orange rind and apple juice in a pan and bring to the boil over a low heat. Simmer for 30 minutes, until the apricots are mushy. Cool slightly, then process in a food processor or blender to a purée. Alternatively, rub the mixture through a sieve. Stir in the cinnamon and raisins.

3 Divide the pastry in half, roll out one half on a lightly floured work surface and use to line the base of the prepared tin. Spread the apricot purée over the top and brush the edges with water. Roll out the rest of the dough to fit over the top of the apricot purée. Press down and seal the edges.

4 Prick the top of the pastry with a fork and brush with soya milk. Bake in a preheated oven, 200°C/400°F/Gas Mark 6, for 20–25 minutes or until the pastry is golden. Leave to cool slightly before cutting into 12 bars. Serve warm or cold.

NUTRITION
Calories *198*; Sugars *13 g*; Protein *4 g*;
Carbohydrate *25 g*; Fat *9 g*; Saturates *2 g*

 moderate

 50 mins

 1 hr

🍲 **COOK'S TIP**
These slices will keep in an airtight container for 3–4 days.

This delicious cheesecake has a rich creamy texture, but contains no dairy produce, because it is made with tofu.

Baked Cheesecake

1 Grease an 18-cm/7-inch round loose-bottomed cake tin with margarine.

2 Mix the digestive biscuit crumbs and melted margarine together in a bowl. Press the mixture into the base of the prepared tin.

3 Put the chopped dates, lemon juice, lemon rind and water into a saucepan and bring to the boil over a low heat. Simmer for 5 minutes until the dates are soft, then mash them roughly with a fork.

4 Place the mixture in a blender or food processor, together with the tofu, apple juice, mashed banana and vanilla essence and process until the mixture forms a thick, smooth purée.

5 Pour the tofu purée into the prepared biscuit crumb base and gently smooth the surface with the back of a spoon.

6 Bake in a preheated oven, 180°C/350°F/Gas Mark 4, for 30–40 minutes until lightly golden. Leave to cool in the tin, then leave to chill in the refrigerator before serving.

7 Place the chopped mango in a blender and process until smooth. Serve it as a sauce with the cheesecake.

SERVES 6

1 tbsp vegan margarine, for greasing
125 g/4½ oz digestive biscuits, crushed
4 tbsp vegan margarine, melted
50 g/1¾ oz chopped stoned dates
4 tbsp lemon juice
grated rind of 1 lemon
3 tbsp water
350 g/12 oz firm tofu (drained weight)
150 ml/5 fl oz apple juice
1 banana, mashed
1 tsp vanilla essence
1 mango, peeled, stoned and chopped

NUTRITION
Calories *282*; Sugars *17 g*; Protein *9 g*;
Carbohydrate *29 g*; Fat *15 g*; Saturates *4 g*

moderate

2 hrs 15 mins

45 mins

Any fruits in season can be used in this wholesome pudding. It is suitable for vegans as it contains no dairy produce.

Fruit Crumble

SERVES 6

1 tbsp vegan margarine, for greasing
6 dessert pears, peeled, cored, quartered and sliced
1 tbsp chopped stem ginger
1 tbsp dark muscovado sugar
2 tbsp orange juice

topping
175 g/6 oz plain flour
75 g/2¾ oz vegan margarine, cut into small pieces
25 g/1 oz flaked almonds
25 g/1 oz porridge oats
50 g/1¾ oz dark muscovado sugar
soya custard, to serve

1 Lightly grease a 1.2-litre/2-pint ovenproof dish with vegan margarine.

2 Mix the pears, ginger, muscovado sugar and orange juice together in a large bowl. Spoon the mixture into the prepared dish.

3 To make the crumble topping, sift the flour into a large bowl. Add the vegan margarine and rub it in with your fingertips until the mixture resembles fine breadcrumbs. Stir in the flaked almonds, porridge oats and muscovado sugar. Mix well.

4 Sprinkle the crumble topping evenly over the pear and ginger mixture.

5 Bake in a preheated oven, 190°C/375°F/Gas Mark 5, for 30 minutes or until the topping is golden and the fruit tender. Serve with soya custard.

NUTRITION
Calories *426*; Sugars *37 g*; Protein *8 g*;
Carbohydrate *67 g*; Fat *16 g*; Saturates *4 g*

easy

10 mins

30 mins

🍳 COOK'S TIP

Stir 1 teaspoon ground mixed spice into the crumble mixture at Step 3 for added flavour, if you prefer.

This is a healthy and extremely tasty variation of the classic Victoria sponge cake, and is suitable for vegans.

Eggless Sponge

1 Grease 2 x 20-cm/8-inch sandwich cake tins with vegan margarine and line the bases with baking paper.

2 Sift the flour and baking powder into a large bowl, stirring in any bran remaining in the sieve. Stir in the caster sugar.

3 Pour in the sunflower oil, water and vanilla essence. Mix well for 1 minute or until the mixture is smooth, then divide between the prepared tins.

4 Bake in a preheated oven, 180°C/350°F/Gas Mark 4, for 25–30 minutes or until just firm to the touch.

5 Leave the sponges to cool in the tins before turning out and transferring to a wire rack to cool completely.

6 To serve, remove the baking paper and place one of the sponges on a serving plate. Cover with the strawberry jam or spread and place the other sponge on top. Dust the cake with a little caster sugar before serving.

SERVES 8

1 tbsp vegan margarine, for greasing
225 g/8 oz self-raising wholemeal flour
2 tsp baking powder
175 g/6 oz caster sugar, plus extra for dusting
6 tbsp sunflower oil
250 ml/8 fl oz water
1 tsp vanilla essence
4 tbsp strawberry or raspberry reduced-sugar spread
caster sugar, for dusting

NUTRITION
Calories 273; Sugars 27 g; Protein 3 g; Carbohydrate 49 g; Fat 9 g; Saturates 1 g

easy

1 hr 15 mins

30 mins

COOK'S TIP

To make a chocolate-flavoured sponge, replace 15 g/½ oz of the flour with sifted cocoa powder. To make a citrus-flavoured sponge, add the grated rind of ½ lemon or orange to the flour at Step 2.

Desserts

Confirmed pudding lovers feel a meal is lacking if there isn't a tempting dessert to finish off the menu. Yet it is often possible to combine indulgence with healthy ingredients. A lot of the recipes in this chapter contain fruit, which is the perfect ingredient for healthy desserts that are still deliciously tempting, such as Blackberry Pudding, Raspberry Shortcake, One-roll Fruit Pie, Apple Tart Tatin and Baked Bananas. Some desserts are also packed full of protein-rich nuts, such as Apricot and Cranberry Tart and Almond Cheesecakes.

A slightly different version of this old favourite, made with the addition of marmalade and orange rind to give a delicious citrus flavour.

Queen *of* Puddings

SERVES 8

2 tbsp butter, plus extra for greasing
600 ml/1 pint milk
225 g/8 oz caster sugar
finely grated rind of 1 orange
4 eggs, separated
75 g/2¾ oz fresh breadcrumbs
6 tbsp orange marmalade
salt

1 Grease a 1.5-litre/2¾-pint ovenproof dish with butter.

2 To make the custard, heat the milk in a saucepan with the butter, 50 g/1¾ oz of the caster sugar and the orange rind over low heat until just warm.

3 Whisk the egg yolks in a bowl. Gradually pour the warm milk over the eggs, whisking constantly.

4 Stir the breadcrumbs into the pan, then transfer the mixture to the prepared dish and leave to stand for 15 minutes.

5 Bake in a preheated oven, 180°C/350°F/Gas Mark 4, for 20–25 minutes or until the custard has just set. Remove from the oven but do not turn the oven off.

6 To make the meringue, whisk the egg whites with a pinch of salt until they stand in soft peaks. Whisk in the remaining caster sugar, a little at a time.

7 Spread the orange marmalade over the cooked custard, then top with the meringue, spreading it to the edges of the dish.

8 Return to the preheated oven and bake for a further 20 minutes until the meringue is crisp and golden.

🟣 **COOK'S TIP**

If you prefer a crisper meringue, bake the pudding in the oven for an extra 5 minutes.

NUTRITION
Calories *289*; Sugars *46 g*; Protein *6 g*;
Carbohydrate *50 g*; Fat *8 g*; Saturates *4 g*

 moderate

 25 mins

🔵 50 mins

Everyone has their own favourite recipe for this dish. This one has added marmalade and grated apples for a really rich and unique taste.

Bread *and* Butter Pudding

1 Use the butter to grease an ovenproof dish and to spread on the slices of bread, then spread the bread with the marmalade.

2 Place a layer of bread in the base of the dish and sprinkle with the lemon rind, half of the raisins or sultanas, half of the mixed peel, half of the cinnamon, all of the apple and half of the light brown sugar.

3 Add another layer of bread, cutting the slices so that they fit the dish.

4 Sprinkle over most of the remaining raisins or sultanas and the remaining peel, cinnamon and light brown sugar, sprinkling it evenly over the bread. Top with a final layer of bread, again cutting to fit the dish.

5 Lightly beat the eggs and milk together in a bowl. Carefully strain the mixture over the bread. If time allows, leave to stand for 20–30 minutes.

6 Sprinkle the top with the demerara sugar and scatter over the remaining raisins or sultanas. Cook in a preheated oven, 200°C/400°F/Gas Mark 6, for 50–60 minutes or until risen and golden-brown. Serve immediately or leave to cool and serve cold.

SERVES 6

5 tbsp butter, softened
4–5 slices of white or brown bread
4 tbsp chunky orange marmalade
grated rind of 1 lemon
85–125 g/3–4½ oz raisins or sultanas
40 g/1½ oz chopped mixed peel
1 tsp ground cinnamon or mixed spice
1 cooking apple, peeled, cored and coarsely grated
85 g/3 oz light brown sugar
3 eggs
500 ml/18 fl oz milk
2 tbsp demerara sugar

NUTRITION
Calories *427*; Sugars *63 g*; Protein *9 g*; Carbohydrate *74 g*; Fat *13 g*; Saturates *7 g*

 moderate

45 mins

1 hr

This is a popular dessert, which can be adapted to suit all types of fruit if plums are not available.

Plum Cobbler

SERVES 6

1–2 tbsp butter, for greasing
1 kg/2 lb 4 oz plums, stoned and sliced
100 g/3½ oz caster sugar
1 tbsp lemon juice
250 g/9 oz plain flour
2 tsp baking powder
75 g/2¾ oz granulated sugar
1 egg, beaten
150 ml/5 fl oz buttermilk
75 g/2¾ oz butter, melted and cooled
double cream, to serve (optional)

1 Lightly grease a 2-litre/3½-pint ovenproof dish with butter.

2 Mix the plums, caster sugar, lemon juice and 25 g/1 oz of the flour together in a large bowl.

3 Spoon the coated plums into the base of the prepared dish, spreading them out evenly.

4 Sift the remaining flour and the baking powder into a large bowl. Add the granulated sugar and stir well.

5 Add the beaten egg, buttermilk and cooled melted butter. Mix gently to form a soft dough.

6 Place spoonfuls of the dough on top of the fruit mixture until it is almost completely covered.

7 Bake in a preheated oven, 190°C/375°F/Gas Mark 5, for about 35–40 minutes or until golden-brown and bubbling.

8 Serve the pudding piping hot with cream, if liked.

NUTRITION
Calories 430; Sugars 46 g; Protein 7 g;
Carbohydrate 79 g; Fat 12 g; Saturates 7 g

 moderate

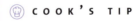 10 mins

40 mins

 COOK'S TIP

If you cannot find buttermilk, try using soured cream.

A delicious dessert to make when blackberries are in abundance. If blackberries are unavailable, try using currants or gooseberries.

Blackberry Pudding

1 Lightly grease a large 850-ml/1½-pint ovenproof dish with butter.

2 Gently mix the blackberries and caster sugar together in a large bowl until the blackberries are well coated in the sugar.

3 Transfer the blackberry and sugar mixture to the prepared dish.

4 Beat the egg and soft brown sugar together in a separate bowl. Stir in the melted butter and milk.

5 Sift the flour into the egg and butter mixture and fold together lightly with a figure-of-eight movement to form a smooth batter.

6 Carefully spread the batter over the blackberry and sugar mixture.

7 Bake the pudding in a preheated oven, 180°C/350°F/Gas Mark 4, for about 25–30 minutes or until the topping is firm and golden.

8 Sprinkle the pudding with a little sugar and serve hot.

SERVES 4

1 tbsp butter, for greasing
450 g/1 lb blackberries
75 g/2¾ oz caster sugar, plus extra for sprinkling
1 egg
75 g/2¾ oz soft brown sugar
6 tbsp butter, melted
8 tbsp milk
125 g/4½ oz self-raising flour

NUTRITION
Calories 455; Sugars 47 g; Protein 7 g; Carbohydrate 70 g; Fat 18 g; Saturates 11 g

  easy

15–20 mins

30 mins

COOK'S TIP

You can add 2 tablespoons of cocoa powder to the batter at Step 5, if you prefer a chocolate flavour.

For this lovely summery dessert, two crisp rounds of shortbread are sandwiched together with fresh raspberries and lightly whipped cream.

Raspberry Shortcake

SERVES 8

100 g/3½ oz butter, cut into cubes, plus extra for greasing

175 g/6 oz self-raising flour, plus extra for dusting

75 g/2¾ oz caster sugar

1 egg yolk

1 tbsp rose water

600 ml/1 pint double cream, whipped lightly

225 g/8 oz raspberries, plus a few extra for decoration

icing sugar, for dusting

1 Lightly grease 2 baking trays with a little butter.

2 To make the shortcake, sift the flour into a large bowl. Add the butter and rub in with your fingertips until the mixture resembles breadcrumbs.

3 Stir the sugar, egg yolk and rose water into the mixture and bring together with your fingers to form a soft dough. Divide the dough in half.

4 Roll out each piece of dough on a lightly floured work surface to a 20-cm/ 8-inch round. Carefully lift each one with the rolling pin on to a prepared baking tray. Crimp the edges of the dough.

5 Bake in a preheated oven, 190°C/375°F/Gas Mark 5, for 15 minutes or until lightly golden. Transfer the shortcakes to a wire rack and leave to cool.

6 Mix the whipped cream and the raspberries together, then spoon the mixture on top of one of the shortcakes, spreading it out evenly. Top with the other shortcake round, dust with a little icing sugar and decorate with the extra raspberries.

NUTRITION

Calories *496*; Sugars *14 g*; Protein *4 g*; Carbohydrate *30 g*; Fat *41 g*; Saturates *26 g*

easy

40 mins

15 mins

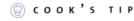 **COOK'S TIP**

The shortcake can be made a few days in advance and stored in an airtight container until required. Add the filling just before serving.

This delicious dessert originated in Australia. Serve it with sharp fruits to balance the sweetness of the meringue.

Pavlova

1 Line a baking sheet with a sheet of baking paper.

2 Whisk the egg whites with a pinch of salt in a large bowl until they form soft peaks.

3 Whisk in the sugar, a little at a time, whisking well after each addition until all the sugar has been incorporated and the meringue is smooth and glossy.

4 Spoon three-quarters of the meringue on to the prepared baking sheet, forming a round 20 cm/8 inches in diameter.

5 Place spoonfuls of the remaining meringue all around the edge of the round to make a nest shape.

6 Bake in a preheated oven, 140°C/275°F/Gas Mark 1, for 1¼ hours.

7 Turn the heat off but leave the pavlova in the oven until it is completely cold.

8 To serve, place the pavlova on a serving dish. Spread with the lightly whipped cream, then arrange the fresh fruit on top. Do not decorate the pavlova too far in advance or it will go soggy.

SERVES 6

3 egg whites
175 g/6 oz caster sugar
300 ml/10 fl oz double cream, whipped lightly
fresh fruit of your choice (raspberries, strawberries, peaches, passion fruit, or cape gooseberries)
salt

 COOK'S TIP

If you are worried about making the round shape, draw a circle on the baking paper, turn the paper over, then spoon the meringue inside the outline.

NUTRITION
Calories *354*; Sugars *34 g*; Protein *3 g*; Carbohydrate *34 g*; Fat *24 g*; Saturates *15 g*

⭐⭐⭐   moderate

🟢   1 hr 10 mins

🕐   1 hr 15 mins

This is an easy way to make a pie, once you have rolled out the pastry and filled it with fruit you just turn the edges of the pastry in!

One-roll Fruit Pie

SERVES 8

pastry
100 g/3½ oz butter, cut into small pieces, plus extra for greasing
175 g/6 oz plain flour, plus extra for dusting
1 tbsp water
1 egg, separated
sugar cubes, crushed, for sprinkling

filling
600 g/1 lb 5 oz prepared fruit (rhubarb, gooseberries, plums, or damsons)
85 g/3 oz soft brown sugar
1 tbsp ground ginger

NUTRITION
Calories 229; Sugars 13 g; Protein 4 g; Carbohydrate 30 g; Fat 11 g; Saturates 7 g

easy

45 mins

35 mins

1 Grease a large baking sheet with a little butter.

2 To make the pastry, sift the flour into a large bowl. Add the butter and rub it in with your fingertips until the mixture resembles breadcrumbs. Add the water and mix to form a soft dough. Wrap in clingfilm and leave to chill in the refrigerator for 30 minutes.

3 Roll out the chilled pastry on a lightly floured work surface, to a round about 35 cm/14 inches in diameter.

4 Transfer the round to the centre of the greased baking tray. Lightly fork the egg yolk and brush it over the pastry.

5 To make the filling, mix the prepared fruit with the brown sugar and ground ginger and pile it into the centre of the pastry.

6 Turn in the edges of the pastry all the way around. Brush the surface of the pastry with the egg white and sprinkle with the crushed sugar cubes.

7 Bake in a preheated oven, 200°C/400°F/Gas Mark 6, for 35 minutes or until golden-brown. Transfer to a serving plate and serve warm.

COOK'S TIP

If the pastry breaks when shaping it into a round, don't panic – just patch and seal, as the overall effect of this tart is rough.

This classic, French upside-down tart is always a popular choice for a comforting dessert at any time of year.

Apple Tart Tatin

1 Heat the butter and sugar in a 23-cm/9-inch ovenproof frying pan over a medium heat for about 5 minutes until the mixture is just beginning to caramelize. Remove the frying pan from the heat.

2 Arrange the apple quarters, skin side down, in the pan, taking care as the butter and sugar will be very hot. Place the frying pan back on the heat and simmer for 2 minutes.

3 Roll out the pastry on a lightly floured work surface, to form a circle just a little larger than the pan.

4 Place the pastry over the apples, press down and carefully tuck in the edges to seal the apples under the layer of pastry.

5 Bake in a preheated oven, 200°C/400°F/Gas Mark 6, for 20–25 minutes or until the pastry is golden. Remove from the oven and leave to cool for about 10 minutes.

6 Place a serving plate over the frying pan and invert so that the pastry forms the base of the tart. Serve warm with crème fraîche.

SERVES 8

125 g/4½ oz butter
125 g/4½ oz caster sugar
4 dessert apples, cored and quartered
250 g/9 oz fresh ready-made shortcrust pastry
plain flour, for dusting
crème fraîche, to serve

NUTRITION
Calories 340; Sugars 23 g; Protein 2 g; Carbohydrate 37 g; Fat 22 g; Saturates 12 g

easy
15 mins
30 mins

COOK'S TIP

Replace the apples with pears, if you prefer. Leave the skin on the pears, cut them into quarters and then remove the core.

This is an old-fashioned pudding, which still delights people time after time. It is very quick to make if you use ready-made pastry.

Treacle Tart

SERVES 8

250 g/9 oz fresh ready-made shortcrust pastry
plain flour, for dusting
350 g/12 oz golden syrup
125 g/4½ oz fresh white breadcrumbs
125 ml/4 fl oz double cream
finely grated rind of ½ lemon or orange
2 tbsp lemon or orange juice
custard, to serve (optional)

1 Roll out the pastry on a lightly floured work surface and use to line a 20-cm/8-inch loose-bottomed quiche/flan tin. Reserve the pastry trimmings. Prick the base of the pastry with a fork and leave to chill in the refrigerator for 30 minutes.

2 Cut out small shapes from the reserved pastry trimmings, such as leaves, stars or hearts, to decorate the top of the tart.

3 Mix the golden syrup, breadcrumbs, cream and grated lemon or orange rind and lemon or orange juice together in a bowl.

4 Pour the mixture into the pastry case and decorate the edges of the tart with the pastry cut-outs.

5 Bake in a preheated oven, 190°C/375°F/Gas Mark 5, for 35–40 minutes or until the filling is just set.

6 Leave the tart to cool slightly in the tin. Turn out on to a serving plate and serve warm with custard, if liked.

NUTRITION
Calories *378*; Sugars *36 g*; Protein *4 g*;
Carbohydrate *57 g*; Fat *17 g*; Saturates *8 g*

easy

50 mins

40 mins

🍲 **COOK'S TIP**

Use the pastry trimmings to create a decorative lattice pattern on top of the tart, if you prefer.

This is a classic egg custard tart, which should be served as fresh as possible for the very best flavour and texture.

Custard Tart

1 To make the pastry, sift the flour into a large bowl, then add the sugar. Add the butter and rub it in with your fingertips until the mixture resembles breadcrumbs. Add the water and mix to form a soft dough. Wrap in clingfilm and leave to chill in the refrigerator for about 30 minutes.

2 Roll out the dough on a lightly floured work surface to form a round slightly larger than a 24-cm/9½-inch loose-bottomed quiche/flan tin and use to line the tin, trimming off any edges. Prick the pastry with a fork and leave to chill in the refrigerator for about 30 minutes.

3 Line the pastry case with foil and baking beans and bake in a preheated oven, 190°C/375°F/Gas Mark 5, for 15 minutes. Remove the foil and baking beans and bake the pastry case for a further 15 minutes.

4 To make the filling, whisk the eggs, cream, milk and nutmeg together in a bowl. Pour the filling into the prepared pastry case. Return the tart to the oven and cook for 25–30 minutes or until the filling is just set. Serve warm.

SERVES 8

pastry
150 g/5½ oz plain flour, plus extra for dusting
25 g/1 oz caster sugar
125 g/4½ oz butter, cut into small pieces
1 tbsp water

filling
3 eggs
150 ml/5 fl oz single cream
150 ml/5 fl oz milk
freshly grated nutmeg

NUTRITION
Calories *268*; Sugars *5 g*; Protein *5 g*; Carbohydrate *20 g*; Fat *19 g*; Saturates *12 g*

easy
1 hr 15 mins
1 hr

 COOK'S TIP

Baking the pastry case blind ensures that the finished tart has a crisp base.

BAKING

No-one will be able to resist this delicious tart with its buttery pastry and a sharp, melt-in-the-mouth lemon filling.

Lemon Tart

SERVES 8

pastry
150 g/5½ oz plain flour, plus extra
   for dusting
25 g/1 oz caster sugar
125 g/4½ oz butter, cut into small pieces
1 tbsp water

filling
150 ml/5 fl oz double cream
100 g/3½ oz caster sugar
4 eggs
grated rind of 3 lemons
175 ml/6 fl oz lemon juice
icing sugar, for dusting
redcurrants, to decorate

1 To make the pastry, sift the flour into a large bowl, then add the sugar. Add the butter and rub it in with your fingertips until the mixture resembles breadcrumbs. Add the water and mix to form a soft dough. Wrap in clingfilm and leave to chill in the refrigerator for 30 minutes.

2 Roll out the dough on a lightly floured work surface and use to line a 24-cm/9½-inch loose-bottomed quiche/flan tin. Prick the pastry with a fork and leave to chill in the refrigerator for 30 minutes.

3 Line the pastry case with foil and baking beans and bake in a preheated oven, 190°C/375°F/Gas Mark 5, for 15 minutes. Remove the foil and baking beans and cook the pastry case for a further 15 minutes.

4 To make the filling, whisk the cream, sugar, eggs, lemon rind and juice together until thoroughly combined. Place the pastry case, still in its tin, on a baking tray and pour in the filling (see Cook's Tip).

5 Bake the tart in the preheated oven for about 20 minutes or until the filling is just set. Leave to cool, then remove the tart from the tin and dust lightly with icing sugar. Decorate with a few redcurrants and serve.

NUTRITION
Calories *363*; Sugars *18 g*; Protein *5 g*;
Carbohydrate *32 g*; Fat *25 g*; Saturates *15 g*

moderate

1 hr 50 mins

50 mins

🍴 **COOK'S TIP**

To avoid any spillage, pour half of the filling into the pastry case, place in the oven and pour in the remaining filling.

This is a variation of the classic lemon tart – in this recipe fresh breadcrumbs are used to create a much thicker texture.

Orange Tart

1 To make the pastry, sift the flour into a large bowl, then add the sugar. Add the butter and rub it in with your fingertips until the mixture resembles breadcrumbs. Add the water and mix to form a soft dough. Wrap in clingfilm and leave to chill in the refrigerator for 30 minutes.

2 Roll out the dough on a lightly floured work surface and use to line a 24-cm/9½-inch loose-bottomed quiche/flan tin. Prick the pastry with a fork and leave to chill in the refrigerator for 30 minutes.

3 Line the pastry case with foil and baking beans and bake in a preheated oven, 190°C/375°F/Gas Mark 5, for 15 minutes. Remove the foil and beans and cook for a further 15 minutes.

4 To make the filling, mix the orange rind and juice and the breadcrumbs together in a bowl. Stir in the lemon juice and cream. Melt the butter and sugar in a saucepan over a low heat. Remove the pan from the heat, add the egg yolks, a pinch of salt and the breadcrumb mixture and stir.

5 Whisk the egg whites with a pinch of salt in a clean bowl until they form soft peaks. Fold them into the egg yolk mixture.

6 Pour the filling into the prepared pastry case and bake in a preheated oven, 160°C/325°F/Gas Mark 3, for about 45 minutes or until just set. Leave to cool slightly and serve warm with a spoonful of crème fraîche decorated with a few strips of orange rind.

SERVES 6 – 8

pastry
150 g/5½ oz plain flour, plus extra
    for dusting
25 g/1 oz caster sugar
125 g/4½ oz butter, cut into small pieces
1 tbsp water

filling
grated rind of 2 oranges, plus extra for
    decoration
135 ml/4½ fl oz orange juice
50 g/1¾ oz fresh white breadcrumbs
2 tbsp lemon juice
150 ml/5 fl oz single cream
4 tbsp butter
50 g/1¾ oz caster sugar
2 eggs, separated
salt
crème fraîche, to serve
strips of orange rind, to decorate

NUTRITION
Calories *450*; Sugars *17 g*; Protein *6 g*;
Carbohydrate *40 g*; Fat *31 g*; Saturates *19 g*

easy

1 hr 20 mins

1 hr 45 mins

This frangipane tart is ideal for Christmas, when fresh cranberries are in abundance. If liked, brush the warm tart with melted apricot jam.

Apricot *and* Cranberry Tart

SERVES 8

pastry
150 g/5½ oz plain flour, plus extra
    for dusting
25 g/1 oz caster sugar
125 g/4½ oz butter, cut into small pieces
1 tbsp water

filling
200 g/7 oz unsalted butter
200 g/7 oz caster sugar
1 egg
2 egg yolks
5 tbsp plain flour, sifted
175 g/6 oz ground almonds
4 tbsp double cream
410 g/14½ oz canned apricot halves, drained
125 g/4½ oz fresh cranberries

NUTRITION
Calories 752; Sugars 40 g; Protein 9 g;
Carbohydrate 59 g; Fat 55 g; Saturates 28 g

🟊🟊🟊   moderate
                1 hr 20 mins
                1 hr 30 mins

1 To make the pastry, sift the flour into a bowl, then add the sugar. Add the butter and rub it in with your fingertips until the mixture resembles breadcrumbs. Add the water and mix to form a soft dough. Wrap in clingfilm and leave to chill in the refrigerator for 30 minutes.

2 Roll out the dough on a lightly floured work surface and use to line a 24-cm/9½-inch loose-bottomed quiche/flan tin. Prick the base of the pastry case all over with a fork and leave to chill in the refrigerator for 30 minutes.

3 Line the pastry case with foil and baking beans and bake in a preheated oven, 190°C/375°F/Gas Mark 5, for 15 minutes. Remove the foil and baking beans and cook the pastry case for a further 10 minutes.

4 To make the filling, cream the butter and sugar together in a bowl until light and fluffy. Beat in the egg and egg yolks, then stir in the flour, ground almonds and cream.

5 Arrange the apricot halves and cranberries over the base of the pastry case and spoon the filling over the top.

6 Bake in the preheated oven for about 1 hour or until the topping is just set. Leave to cool slightly, then serve warm or cold.

These tarts are made with ready-made puff pastry, which is available from most supermarkets. The finished pastry is very rich and buttery.

Pear Tarts

1 Roll out the pastry on a lightly floured work surface. Cut out 6 x 10-cm/ 4-inch rounds with a plain cutter.

2 Place the rounds on a large baking tray and leave to chill in the refrigerator for 30 minutes.

3 Cream the brown sugar and butter together in a small bowl, then stir in the chopped stem ginger.

4 Prick the pastry rounds with a fork and spread a little of the ginger mixture on to each one.

5 Slice the pear halves lengthways, keeping the pears intact at the tip. Fan out the slices slightly.

6 Place a fanned-out pear half on top of each pastry round. Make small flutes around the edge of the pastry rounds and brush each pear half with a little melted butter.

7 Bake in a preheated oven, 200°C/400°F/Gas Mark 6, for 15–20 minutes or until the pastry is risen and golden. Leave to cool slightly, then serve warm.

COOK'S TIP

Serve these tarts with a spoonful of whipped cream or vanilla ice cream for a delicious dessert.

SERVES 6

250 g/9 oz fresh ready-made puff pastry
plain flour, for dusting
25 g/1 oz soft brown sugar
2 tbsp butter, plus extra for brushing
1 tbsp finely chopped stem ginger
3 pears, peeled, halved and cored

NUTRITION
Calories 250; Sugars 15 g; Protein 3 g;
Carbohydrate 30 g; Fat 14 g; Saturates 3 g

easy

35 mins

20 mins

Serve these unusual, melt-in-the-mouth tarts with fresh mixed summer berries, if liked.

Crème Brûlée Tarts

SERVES 6

pastry
150 g/5½ oz plain flour, plus extra for dusting
25 g/1 oz caster sugar
125 g/4½ oz butter, cut into small pieces
1 tbsp water

filling
4 egg yolks
50 g/1¾ oz caster sugar
400 ml/14 fl oz double cream
1 tsp vanilla essence
demerara sugar, for sprinkling
mixed fresh berries, to serve

NUTRITION
Calories *635*; Sugars *17 g*; Protein *6 g*; Carbohydrate *36 g*; Fat *53 g*; Saturates *32 g*

easy

16 hrs 20 mins

25 mins

1 To make the pastry, sift the flour into a bowl, then add the sugar. Add the butter and rub it in with your fingertips until the mixture resembles breadcrumbs. Add the water and mix to form a soft dough. Wrap in clingfilm and leave to chill in the refrigerator for 30 minutes.

2 Divide the dough into 6 pieces. Roll out each piece on a lightly floured work surface and use to line 6 tart tins, each 10 cm/4 inches wide. Prick the base of the pastry with a fork and leave to chill in the refrigerator for 20 minutes.

3 Line the pastry cases with foil and baking beans and bake in a preheated oven, 190°C/375°F/Gas Mark 5, for 15 minutes. Remove the foil and beans and cook the pastry cases for a further 10 minutes until crisp. Leave to cool.

4 Meanwhile, make the filling. Beat the egg yolks and sugar together in a bowl until pale. Heat the cream and vanilla essence in a saucepan until just below boiling point, then pour it on to the egg mixture, whisking constantly.

5 Return the mixture to a clean pan and bring to just below the boil, stirring constantly, until thick. Do not allow the mixture to boil or it will curdle.

6 Leave the mixture to cool slightly, then pour it into the tart tins. Leave to cool and then chill in the refrigerator overnight.

7 Sprinkle the tarts with demerara sugar. Place under a preheated hot grill for a few minutes. Leave to cool, then chill in the refrigerator for 2 hours before serving. Serve with mixed fresh berries.

These creamy cheese desserts are so delicious that it is hard to believe that they are low in fat.

Almond Cheesecakes

1 Place the biscuits in a clean plastic bag, seal the bag and, using a rolling pin, crush them into small pieces.

2 Place the crumbs in a bowl and stir in the egg white to bind them together.

3 Arrange 4 non-stick pastry rings or poached egg rings, 9 cm/3½ inches across, on a baking tray lined with baking paper. Divide the biscuit mixture into 4 equal portions and spoon it into the rings, pressing down well. Bake in a preheated oven, 180°C/350°F/Gas Mark 4, for 10 minutes or until crisp. Remove from the oven and leave to cool in the rings.

4 Beat the soft cheese, then beat in the almond essence, lime rind, ground almonds, sugar and sultanas until well mixed.

5 Dissolve the gelatine in the boiling water and stir in the lime juice. Fold into the cheese mixture and spoon over the biscuit bases. Smooth over the tops and leave to chill in the refrigerator for 1 hour or until set.

6 Loosen the cheesecakes from the tins with a small palette knife or spatula and transfer to serving plates. Decorate with flaked toasted almonds and strips of lime rind and serve.

SERVES 4

12 amaretti biscuits
1 egg white, beaten lightly
225 g/8 oz skimmed milk soft cheese
½ tsp almond essence
½ tsp finely grated lime rind
25 g/1 oz ground almonds
25 g/1 oz caster sugar
55 g/2 oz sultanas
2 tsp powdered gelatine
2 tbsp boiling water
2 tbsp lime juice

to decorate
25 g/1 oz flaked toasted almonds
strips of lime rind

NUTRITION
Calories *361*; Sugars *29 g*; Protein *16 g*;
Carbohydrate *43 g*; Fat *15 g*; Saturates *4 g*

easy

1 hr 15 mins

10 mins

This simple combination of fudgy meringue topped with fromage frais and raspberries is the perfect finale to any meal.

Brown Sugar Pavlovas

SERVES 4

2 large egg whites
1 tsp cornflour
1 tsp raspberry vinegar
100 g/3½ oz light muscovado sugar, crushed free of lumps
2 tbsp redcurrant jelly
2 tbsp unsweetened orange juice
150 ml/5 fl oz low-fat fromage frais
175 g/6 oz raspberries, thawed if frozen
rose-scented geranium leaves, to decorate (optional)

1 Line a large baking tray with baking paper. Whisk the egg whites until very stiff and dry. Gently fold in the cornflour and vinegar.

2 Gradually whisk in the sugar, a spoonful at a time, until the mixture is thick and glossy.

3 Divide the mixture into 4 portions and spoon on to the prepared baking tray, spaced well apart. Smooth each portion into a round, about 10 cm/4 inches across and bake in a preheated oven, 150°C/300°C/Gas Mark 2, for about 40–45 minutes or until lightly browned and crisp. Remove from the oven and leave to cool on the baking tray.

4 Place the redcurrant jelly and orange juice in a small saucepan and heat, stirring constantly, until melted. Leave to cool for 10 minutes.

5 Using a palette knife, carefully remove each pavlova from the baking paper and transfer to 4 serving plates. Top with the fromage frais and raspberries. Brush the fruit with the redcurrant and orange glaze and decorate with the geranium leaves, if using.

NUTRITION
Calories 155; Sugars 34 g; Protein 5 g;
Carbohydrate 35 g; Fat 0.2 g; Saturates 0 g

      easy

🌱   1 hr

🕐   1 hr

🍳 **COOK'S TIP**

Make a large pavlova by forming the meringue into a single round, measuring 18 cm/7 inches across, on a lined baking tray. Bake in a preheated oven for 1 hour.

This simple, healthy recipe is easy to prepare and cook, but is deliciously warming. For a treat, serve hot on a pool of low-fat custard.

Baked Pears *with* Cinnamon

1 Core and peel the pears, then slice them in half lengthways and brush them all over with the lemon juice to prevent them from discolouring. Place the pears, cored side down, in a small non-stick roasting tin.

2 Place the sugar, cinnamon and low-fat spread in a small saucepan and heat gently, stirring constantly, until the sugar has dissolved. Keep the heat very low to stop too much water evaporating from the low-fat spread as it gets hot. Spoon the mixture over the pears.

3 Bake in a preheated oven, 200°C/400°F/Gas Mark 6, for 20–25 minutes or until they are tender and golden, occasionally spooning the sugar mixture over the fruit during the cooking time.

4 To serve, heat the custard until piping hot and spoon a little over the base of each of 4 warmed dessert plates. Arrange 2 pear halves on each plate.

5 Decorate the pears with shredded lemon rind and serve with extra custard.

SERVES 4

4 ripe pears
2 tbsp lemon juice
4 tbsp light muscovado sugar
1 tsp ground cinnamon
55 g/2 oz low-fat spread
600 ml/1 pint low-fat custard
finely shredded lemon rind, to decorate
low-fat custard, to serve

NUTRITION
Calories 207; Sugars 35 g; Protein 3 g; Carbohydrate 37 g; Fat 6 g; Saturates 2 g

easy
10 mins
25 mins

🍴 COOK'S TIP

For alternative flavours, replace the cinnamon with ground ginger and serve the pears sprinkled with chopped stem ginger in syrup. Alternatively, use ground allspice and spoon over some warmed dark rum to serve.

The orange-flavoured cream can be prepared in advance but do not make up the banana parcels until just before you need to cook them.

Baked Bananas

SERVES 4

4 bananas
2 passion fruit
4 tbsp orange juice
4 tbsp orange-flavoured liqueur

orange-flavoured cream
150 ml/5 fl oz double cream
3 tbsp icing sugar
2 tbsp orange-flavoured liqueur

1 To make the orange-flavoured cream, pour the cream into a large bowl and sprinkle over the icing sugar. Whisk the mixture until it is standing in soft peaks. Carefully fold in the orange-flavoured liqueur and leave to chill in the refrigerator until required.

2 Peel the bananas and place each one on to a sheet of foil.

3 Cut the passion fruit in half and squeeze the juice of each half over each banana. Spoon over the orange juice and liqueur.

4 Fold the foil over the top of the bananas, tucking the ends in, so they are completely enclosed.

5 Place the parcels on a baking tray and bake the bananas in a preheated oven, 180°C/350°F/Gas Mark 4, for about 10 minutes or until the bananas are just tender. Check by piercing the foil parcel with a cocktail stick.

6 Transfer the foil parcels to 4 warmed serving plates. Open out the foil parcels at the table and serve with the chilled orange-flavoured cream.

NUTRITION
Calories *380* Sugars *40 g*; Protein *2 g*;
Carbohydrate *43 g*; Fat *18 g*; Saturates *11 g*

easy

30 mins

10 mins

 COOK'S TIP

Leave the bananas in their skins for a really quick dessert. Split the banana skins and pop in 1–2 cubes of chocolate. Wrap the bananas in foil and bake in a preheated oven for 10 minutes or until the chocolate just melts.

This winter dessert is a classic dish. Large, fluffy apples are hollowed out and filled with spices, almonds and blackberries.

Baked Apples *with* Berries

1 Using a small, sharp knife, make a shallow cut through the skin around the centre of each apple – this will help the apples to cook through.

2 Core the apples, brush the centres with the lemon juice to prevent them from discolouring and stand them in an ovenproof dish.

3 Mix the blackberries, almonds, allspice, lemon rind and sugar together in a bowl. Using a teaspoon, spoon the mixture into the centre of each apple.

4 Pour the port into the dish, add the cinnamon stick and bake the apples in a preheated oven, 200°C/400°F/Gas Mark 6, for 35–40 minutes or until tender and softened.

5 Drain the cooking juices into a saucepan and set over a low heat. Keep the apples warm.

6 Discard the cinnamon and add the cornflour mixture to the pan. Cook, stirring constantly, until thickened.

7 Heat the custard in a small pan until piping hot. Pour the sauce over the apples and serve with the custard.

SERVES 4

4 medium cooking apples
1 tbsp lemon juice
100 g/3½ oz prepared blackberries, thawed if frozen
15 g/½ oz flaked almonds
½ tsp ground allspice
½ tsp finely grated lemon rind
2 tbsp demerara sugar
300 ml/10 fl oz ruby port
1 cinnamon stick, broken
2 tsp cornflour blended with 2 tbsp cold water
600 ml/1 pint low-fat custard, to serve

NUTRITION

Calories *228*; Sugars *31 g*; Protein *1 g*; Carbohydrate *31 g*; Fat *2 g*; Saturates *0.2 g*

easy

10 mins

 50 mins

This rich pudding is cooked with cream and apples and delicately flavoured with orange.

Italian Bread Pudding

SERVES 4

1 tbsp butter, for greasing

2 small eating apples, peeled, cored and sliced into rings

75 g/2¾ oz granulated sugar

2 tbsp white wine

100 g/3½ oz bread, sliced with crusts removed (slightly stale French baguette is ideal)

300 ml/10 fl oz single cream

2 eggs, beaten

pared rind of 1 orange, cut into matchsticks

1 Lightly grease a 1.2-litre/2-pint deep ovenproof dish with the butter.

2 Arrange the apple rings in the base of the prepared dish and sprinkle over half of the sugar.

3 Pour the wine over the apples. Add the bread slices, pushing them down with your hands to flatten them slightly.

4 Mix the cream, eggs, the remaining sugar and the orange rind in a small bowl and pour the mixture over the bread. Leave to soak for 30 minutes.

5 Bake in a preheated oven, 180°C/350°F/Gas Mark 4, for 25 minutes until golden and set. Remove from the oven, leave to cool slightly and serve warm.

NUTRITION

Calories 387; Sugars 31 g; Protein 8 g; Carbohydrate 45 g; Fat 20 g; Saturates 12 g

 easy

45 mins

25 mins

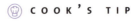 **COOK'S TIP**

For a change, try adding dried fruit, such as apricots, cherries or dates, to the pudding.

These baked mini ricotta puddings are delicious served warm or chilled and will keep in the refrigerator for 3–4 days.

Tuscan Pudding

1 Lightly grease 4 mini pudding basins or ramekin dishes with butter.

2 Put the dried fruit in a bowl and cover with warm water. Leave to soak for about 10 minutes.

3 Beat the ricotta cheese and egg yolks together in a bowl. Stir in the caster sugar, cinnamon and orange rind and mix well.

4 Drain the dried fruit in a sieve set over a bowl. Mix the drained fruit with the ricotta cheese mixture.

5 Spoon the mixture into the prepared basins or ramekin dishes.

6 Bake in a preheated oven, 180°C/350°F/Gas Mark 4, for 15 minutes. The tops should be firm to the touch but should not have turned brown.

7 Decorate the puddings with grated orange rind. Serve warm or chilled with a spoonful of crème fraîche, if liked.

SERVES 4

1 tbsp butter, for greasing
75 g/2¾ oz mixed dried fruit
250 g/9 oz ricotta cheese
3 egg yolks
50 g/1¾ oz caster sugar
1 tsp cinnamon
finely grated rind of 1 orange, plus extra
    to decorate
crème fraîche, to serve (optional)

NUTRITION
Calories *293*; Sugars *28 g*; Protein *9 g*;
Carbohydrate *28 g*; Fat *17 g*; Saturates *9 g*

easy

20 mins

15 mins

 COOK'S TIP

Crème fraîche has a slightly sour, nutty taste and is very thick. It is suitable for cooking, but has the same fat content as double cream. It can be made by stirring cultured buttermilk into double cream and refrigerating overnight.

The lemon and mascarpone give this baked cheesecake a wonderfully tangy flavour. Ricotta cheese could be used as an alternative.

Mascarpone Cheesecake

SERVES 8

1½ tbsp unsalted butter, plus extra for greasing
150 g/5½ oz ginger biscuits, crushed
25 g/1 oz stem ginger, chopped
500 g/1 lb 2 oz mascarpone cheese
finely grated rind and juice of 2 lemons
100 g/3½ oz caster sugar
2 large eggs, separated
fruit coulis (see Cook's Tip), to serve

1 Grease the base of a 25-cm/10-inch spring-form cake tin or loose-bottomed tin with butter and line the base with baking paper.

2 Melt the butter in a saucepan over a low heat and stir in the crushed biscuits and chopped ginger. Use the mixture to line the tin, pressing the mixture about 5 mm/¼ inch up the sides.

3 Beat the mascarpone cheese, lemon rind and juice, sugar and egg yolks together in a bowl until quite smooth.

4 Whisk the egg whites in a clean bowl until stiff, then fold into the cheese and lemon mixture.

5 Pour the mixture into the prepared tin and bake in a preheated oven, 180°C/350°F/Gas Mark 4, for 35–45 minutes or until just set. Don't worry if it cracks or sinks – this is quite normal. Leave the cheesecake to cool in the tin, then serve with a fruit coulis (see Cook's Tip).

NUTRITION
Calories 327; Sugars 25 g; Protein 9 g; Carbohydrate 33 g; Fat 18 g; Saturates 11 g

⭐⭐⭐ moderate
🕐 15 mins
🕐 50 mins

 COOK'S TIP

Fruit coulis can be made by cooking 400 g/14 oz fruit, such as blueberries, for 5 minutes with 2 tablespoons of water. Sieve the mixture, then stir in 1 tablespoon (or more to taste) of sifted icing sugar. Leave to cool before serving.

These scrumptious little parcels are the perfect dessert for anyone with a sweet tooth and a fancy for something unusual.

Baked Sweet Ravioli

1 To make the sweet pasta dough, sift the flour into a large bowl, then mix in the butter, sugar and 3 of the eggs.

2 Mix the yeast and warm milk together in a small bowl and when thoroughly combined, mix into the dough.

3 Knead the dough for 20 minutes, cover with a clean tea towel and leave in a warm place for 1 hour to rise.

4 To make the filling, mix the chestnut purée, cocoa powder, sugar, almonds, crushed biscuits and orange marmalade together in a separate bowl.

5 Generously grease a baking tray with some butter.

6 Roll out the sweet pasta dough on a lightly floured work surface into a thin sheet and cut into 5-cm/2-inch rounds with a plain pastry cutter.

7 Put a spoonful of filling on to one half of each pasta round and then fold in half, pressing the edges firmly together to seal. Transfer the ravioli to the prepared baking tray, spacing them out well. Bake in batches, if necessary.

8 Beat the remaining egg and brush all over the ravioli to glaze. Bake in a preheated oven, 180°C/350°F/Gas Mark 4, for 20 minutes. Serve hot.

SERVES 4

sweet pasta dough
425 g/15 oz plain flour, plus extra for dusting
140 g/5 oz butter, plus extra for greasing
140 g/5 oz caster sugar
4 eggs
25 g/1 oz yeast
125 ml/4 fl oz warm milk

filling
175 g/6 oz chestnut purée
55 g/2 oz cocoa powder
55 g/2 oz caster sugar
55 g/2 oz chopped almonds
55 g/2 oz crushed amaretti biscuits
175 g/6 oz orange marmalade

NUTRITION
Calories 765; Sugars 56 g; Protein 16 g; Carbohydrate 114 g; Fat 30 g; Saturates 15 g

✪✪✪ moderate

🌱 1 hr 30 mins

 20 mins

Cakes *and* Bread

There is nothing more traditional than afternoon tea and cakes and this chapter gives a wickedly extravagant twist to some of those delicious tea-time classics – full of chocolate, spice and all things nice, these recipes are a treat to enjoy. The chapter includes a variety of different cakes depending on the time you have and the effort you want to spend. Small cakes include Cranberry Muffins, Almond Slices, and Treacle Scones. These cakes are easier to prepare and cook than larger ones and, in general, are particular favourites.

These popular tea snacks are ideal split in half and toasted, then spread with butter. Use a luxury mix of dried fruit, if possible.

Teacakes

MAKES 12 TEACAKES

2 tbsp butter, cut into small pieces, plus extra for greasing
450 g/1 lb strong white bread flour, plus extra for dusting
1 sachet easy-blend dried yeast
50 g/1¾ oz caster sugar
1 tsp salt
300 ml/10 fl oz hand-hot milk
75 g/2¾ oz luxury dried fruit mix
1–2 tbsp honey, for brushing

1 Grease several baking trays with a little butter.

2 Sift the flour into a large bowl. Stir in the dried yeast, sugar and salt. Add the butter and rub it in with your fingertips until the mixture resembles fine breadcrumbs. Add the milk and mix to form a soft dough.

3 Knead the dough on a lightly floured work surface for about 5 minutes. Alternatively, use an electric mixer with a dough hook.

4 Place the dough in a greased bowl, cover and leave to rise in a warm place for about 1–1½ hours or until doubled in size.

5 Knead the dough again for a few minutes and knead in the fruit. Divide the dough into 12 rounds and place on the prepared baking trays. Cover and leave for 1 further hour or until springy to the touch.

6 Bake in a preheated oven, 200°C/400°F/Gas Mark 6, for 20 minutes.

7 Transfer the teacakes to a wire rack and brush with honey while they are still warm. Leave to cool before serving them split in half and toasted, if liked.

NUTRITION
Calories 197; Sugars 11 g; Protein 6 g; Carbohydrate 39 g; Fat 3 g; Saturates 2 g

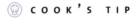

easy

3 hrs 15 mins

20 mins

 COOK'S TIP

It is important to have the milk at the right temperature: heat it until you can put your little finger into the milk and leave it there for 10 seconds without it feeling too hot.

These cinnamon-flavoured buns are delicious if they are served a few minutes after they come out of the oven.

Cinnamon Swirls

1 Grease a 23-cm/9-inch square baking tin with a little butter.

2 Sift the flour and salt into a large bowl. Stir in the dried yeast. Add the butter and rub it in with your fingertips until the mixture resembles fine breadcrumbs. Add the egg and milk and mix to form a dough.

3 Place the dough in a greased bowl, cover and leave to rise in a warm place for about 40 minutes or until doubled in size.

4 Knead the dough lightly for about 1 minute to knock it back, then roll out on a lightly floured work surface to a rectangle 30 x 23 cm/12 x 9 inches.

5 To make the filling, cream the butter, cinnamon and brown sugar together in a bowl until light and fluffy. Spread the filling evenly over the dough, leaving a 2.5-cm/1-inch border all round. Sprinkle over the currants.

6 Roll up the dough like a Swiss roll, starting at a long edge, and press down to seal. Cut the roll into 12 slices. Place them in the prepared tin, cover and leave to stand for 30 minutes.

7 Bake in a preheated oven, 190°C/375°F/Gas Mark 5, for 20–30 minutes or until well risen. Brush the swirls with maple syrup and leave to cool slightly before serving warm.

MAKES 12

2 tbsp butter, cut into small pieces, plus extra for greasing
225 g/8 oz strong white bread flour, plus extra for dusting
½ tsp salt
1 sachet easy-blend dried yeast
1 egg, beaten
125 ml/4 fl oz warm milk
2 tbsp maple syrup

filling
4 tbsp butter, softened
2 tsp ground cinnamon
50 g/1¾ oz soft brown sugar
50 g/1¾ oz currants

NUTRITION
Calories *160*; Sugars *10 g*; Protein *4 g*;
Carbohydrate *24 g*; Fat *6 g*; Saturates *4 g*

⭐⭐⭐ moderate

🕐 1 hr 25 mins

 30 mins

This spicy, fruit tea bread is quick and easy to make. Serve it buttered and with a drizzle of honey for an afternoon snack.

Cinnamon *and* Currant Loaf

MAKES 1 LOAF

150 g/5½ oz butter, cut into small pieces, plus extra for greasing
350 g/12 oz plain flour
pinch of salt
1 tbsp baking powder
1 tbsp ground cinnamon
125 g/4½ oz soft brown sugar
175 g/6 oz currants
finely grated rind of 1 orange
5–6 tbsp orange juice
6 tbsp milk
2 eggs, beaten lightly

1 Grease a 900-g/2-lb loaf tin and line the base with baking paper.

2 Sift the flour, salt, baking powder and ground cinnamon into a large bowl. Add the butter and rub it in with your fingertips until the mixture resembles coarse breadcrumbs.

3 Stir in the sugar, currants and orange rind. Beat the orange juice, milk and eggs together and add to the dry ingredients. Mix well.

4 Spoon the mixture into the prepared tin. Make a slight dip in the centre of the mixture to help it rise evenly.

5 Bake in a preheated oven, 180°C/350°F/Gas Mark 4, for about 1 hour–1 hour 10 minutes or until a fine metal skewer inserted into the centre of the loaf comes out clean.

6 Leave the loaf to cool in the tin before transferring to a wire rack to cool completely before slicing and serving.

NUTRITION
Calories *439*; Sugars *33 g*; Protein *7 g*; Carbohydrate *67 g*; Fat *18 g*; Saturates *11 g*

 moderate

 1 hr 10 mins

1 hr 10 mins

COOK'S TIP

Once you have added the liquid to the dry ingredients, work as quickly as possible because the baking powder is activated by the liquid.

This tea bread is excellent for afternoon tea or coffee time with its moist texture and moreish flavour.

Banana *and* Date Loaf

1 Grease a 900-g/2-lb loaf tin with a little butter and line the base with baking paper.

2 Sift the flour into a large bowl. Add the butter and rub it in with your fingertips until the mixture resembles fine breadcrumbs.

3 Stir in the sugar, chopped dates, bananas, beaten eggs and honey and mix together to form a soft dropping consistency.

4 Spoon the mixture into the prepared loaf tin, spreading it out evenly. Smooth the surface with the back of a knife.

5 Bake in a preheated oven, 160°C/325°F/Gas Mark 3, for about 1 hour or until golden and a fine metal skewer inserted into the centre of the loaf comes out clean.

6 Leave the loaf to cool in the tin before turning out and transferring to a wire rack to cool completely.

7 Serve the loaf warm, cut into thick slices with a few fresh dates, if liked.

COOK'S TIP

This tea bread will keep for several days if stored in an airtight container and kept in a cool, dry place.

MAKES 1 LOAF

100 g/3½ oz butter, cut into small pieces, plus extra for greasing
225 g/8 oz self-raising flour
75 g/2¾ oz caster sugar
125 g/4½ oz stoned dates, chopped
2 bananas, mashed roughly
2 eggs, beaten lightly
2 tbsp honey
fresh dates, to serve (optional)

NUTRITION
Calories *432*; Sugars *41 g*; Protein *7 g*; Carbohydrate *70 g*; Fat *16 g*; Saturates *10 g*

  moderate

  15 mins

1 hr

This bread is full of good things – chopped dates, sesame seeds and honey. Toast thick slices and spread with soft cheese for a light snack.

Date *and* Honey Loaf

MAKES 1 LOAF

1–2 tbsp butter for greasing
250 g/9 oz strong white bread flour, plus extra for dusting
75 g/2¾ oz strong brown bread flour
½ tsp salt
1 sachet easy-blend dried yeast
200 ml/7 fl oz hand-hot water
3 tbsp sunflower oil
3 tbsp honey
75 g/2¾ oz dried dates, chopped
2 tbsp sesame seeds

1 Grease a 900-g/2-lb loaf tin with butter. Sift the white and brown flours into a large bowl and stir in the salt and dried yeast.

2 Pour in the water, sunflower oil and honey and mix to form a dough.

3 Knead the dough on a lightly floured work surface for about 5 minutes or until smooth.

4 Place the dough in a greased bowl, cover and leave to rise in a warm place for about 1 hour or until doubled in size.

5 Knead in the dates and sesame seeds. Shape the dough and place in the tin.

6 Cover and leave in a warm place for a further 30 minutes or until springy to the touch.

7 Bake in a preheated oven, 220°C/425°F/Gas Mark 7, for 30 minutes or until a hollow sound is heard when the base of the loaf is tapped.

8 Transfer the loaf to a wire rack and leave to cool completely. Cut into thick slices and serve.

NUTRITION
Calories *240*; Sugars *14 g*; Protein *6 g*; Carbohydrate *44 g*; Fat *6 g*; Saturates *1 g*

moderate

2 hrs 40 mins

30 mins

COOK'S TIP

If you cannot find a warm place, place the bowl containing the dough over a saucepan of warm water and cover.

The pumpkin purée in this loaf makes it beautifully moist. It is delicious eaten at any time of the day.

Pumpkin Loaf

1 Brush a 900-g/2-lb loaf tin with vegetable oil.

2 Chop the pumpkin into large pieces and wrap in buttered foil. Cook in a preheated oven, 200°C/400°F/Gas Mark 6, for 30–40 minutes or until tender.

3 Leave the pumpkin to cool completely before mashing well with a fork to make a thick purée.

4 Cream the butter and sugar together in a bowl until light and fluffy. Add the beaten eggs a little at a time.

5 Stir in the pumpkin purée, then fold in the flour, baking powder, salt and mixed spice.

6 Fold the pumpkin seeds gently through the mixture, then spoon into the prepared loaf tin.

7 Bake in a preheated oven, 160°C/325°F/Gas Mark 3, for about $1\frac{1}{4}$–$1\frac{1}{2}$ hours or until a skewer inserted into the centre of the loaf comes out clean.

8 Transfer the loaf to a wire rack to cool, then serve.

COOK'S TIP

To ensure that the pumpkin purée is dry, place it in a saucepan over a medium heat for a few minutes, stirring frequently, until it thickens.

MAKES 1 LOAF

1 tbsp vegetable oil for greasing
450 g/1 lb pumpkin flesh
125 g/4½ oz butter, softened, plus extra for greasing
175 g /6 oz caster sugar
2 eggs, beaten
225 g/8 oz plain flour, sifted
1½ tsp baking powder
½ tsp salt
1 tsp ground mixed spice
25 g/1 oz pumpkin seeds

NUTRITION
Calories *456*; Sugars *33 g*; Protein *7 g*; Carbohydrate *62 g*; Fat *21 g*; Saturates *12 g*

easy

1 hr 30 mins

2 hrs 10 mins

The flavours in this bread will bring a touch of sunshine to your breakfast table. The mango can be replaced with other dried fruits.

Tropical Fruit Bread

MAKES 1 LOAF

2 tbsp butter, cut into small pieces, plus extra for greasing
350 g/12 oz strong white bread flour, plus extra for dusting
50 g /1¾ oz bran
½ tsp salt
½ tsp ground ginger
1 sachet easy-blend dried yeast
25 g/1 oz soft brown sugar
250 ml/9 fl oz tepid water
75 g/2¾ oz glacé pineapple, chopped finely
25 g/1 oz dried mango, chopped finely
50 g/1¾ oz desiccated coconut, toasted
1 egg, beaten
2 tbsp coconut shreds

1 Grease a baking tray with butter. Sift the flour into a large bowl. Stir in the bran, salt, ginger, dried yeast and sugar. Add the butter and rub it in with your fingertips, then add the water and mix to form a dough.

2 Knead the dough on a lightly floured work surface for 5–8 minutes or until smooth. Alternatively, use an electric mixer with a dough hook. Place the dough in a greased bowl, cover and leave to rise in a warm place for about 30 minutes or until doubled in size.

3 Knead the pineapple, mango and desiccated coconut into the dough. Shape into a round and place on the baking tray. Score the top with the back of a knife. Cover and leave to rise in a warm place for a further 30 minutes.

4 Brush the loaf with the beaten egg and sprinkle with the 2 tablespoons of coconut shreds. Bake in a preheated oven, 220°C/425°F/Gas Mark 7, for about 30 minutes or until golden-brown on top.

5 Remove the loaf from the oven and transfer to a wire rack to cool before serving in slices.

NUTRITION
Calories *228*; Sugars *10 g*; Protein *6 g*; Carbohydrate *37 g*; Fat *7 g*; Saturates *5 g*

moderate

1 hr 15 mins

30 mins

👑 COOK'S TIP

To test the bread after the second rising, gently poke the dough with your finger – it should spring back if it has risen enough.

This sweet loaf is flavoured with citrus fruits. As with Tropical Fruit Bread (see opposite), it is excellent served at breakfast.

Citrus Bread

1 Lightly grease a baking tray with a little butter.

2 Sift the flour and salt into a large bowl. Stir in the sugar and dried yeast. Add the butter and rub it in with your fingertips until the mixture resembles breadcrumbs. Add the orange, lemon and lime juice, and the water, then mix to form a dough.

3 Knead the dough on a floured work surface for 5 minutes. Alternatively, use an electric mixer with a dough hook. Place the dough in a greased bowl, cover and leave to rise in a warm place for 1 hour or until doubled in size.

4 Meanwhile, grate the rind of the orange, lemon and lime. Knead the fruit rinds into the dough.

5 Divide the dough into 2 balls, making one slightly bigger than the other. Place the larger ball on the baking tray and set the smaller one on top.

6 Push a floured finger through the centre of the dough. Cover and leave to rise for about 40 minutes or until springy to the touch.

7 Bake in a preheated oven, 220°C/425°F/Gas Mark 7, for 35 minutes. Remove from the oven and transfer to a wire rack. Glaze with honey and cool.

MAKES 1 LOAF

4 tbsp butter, cut into small pieces, plus extra for greasing

450 g/1 lb strong white bread flour, plus extra for dusting

½ tsp salt

50 g/1¾ oz caster sugar

1 sachet easy-blend dried yeast

5–6 tbsp orange juice

4 tbsp lemon juice

3–4 tbsp lime juice

150 ml/5 fl oz hand-hot water

1 orange

1 lemon

1 lime

2 tbsp clear honey

NUTRITION
Calories 195; Sugars 10 g; Protein 5 g; Carbohydrate 37 g; Fat 4 g; Saturates 2 g

 moderate

1 hr 55 mins

35 mins

For the chocoholics among us, this bread is not only great fun to make, it is even better to eat.

Chocolate Bread

MAKES 1 LOAF

1 tbsp butter for greasing
450 g/1 lb strong white bread flour, plus extra for dusting
25 g/1 oz cocoa powder
1 tsp salt
1 sachet easy-blend dried yeast
25 g/1 oz soft brown sugar
1 tbsp oil
300 ml/10 fl oz hand-hot water
butter curls, to serve

1 Lightly grease a 900-g/2-lb loaf tin with a little butter.

2 Sift the flour and cocoa powder into a large bowl. Stir in the salt, dried yeast and brown sugar.

3 Pour in the oil along with the water and mix together to form a dough.

4 Knead the dough on a floured work surface for 5 minutes. Alternatively, use an electric mixer with a dough hook.

5 Place the dough in a greased bowl, cover and leave to rise in a warm place for about 1 hour or until it has doubled in size.

6 Knock back the dough and shape it into a loaf. Place the dough in the prepared tin, cover and leave to rise in a warm place for a further 30 minutes.

7 Bake in a preheated oven, 200°C/400°F/Gas Mark 6, for 25–30 minutes or until a hollow sound is heard when the base of the bread is tapped.

8 Transfer the bread to a wire rack and leave to cool. Cut into slices and serve with butter curls.

NUTRITION
Calories 228; Sugars 4 g; Protein 8 g;
Carbohydrate 46 g; Fat 3 g; Saturates 1 g

 moderate

2 hrs 40 mins

30 mins

 COOK'S TIP

This bread can be sliced and spread with butter or it can be lightly toasted.

This is a sweet bread, which has puréed mango mixed into the dough, resulting in a moist loaf with an exotic flavour.

Mango Twist Bread

1 Grease a baking tray with a little butter. Sift the flour and salt into a large bowl, stir in the dried yeast, ground ginger and brown sugar. Add the butter and rub it in with your fingertips until the mixture resembles breadcrumbs. Stir in the mango purée, water and honey and mix to form a dough.

2 Knead the dough on a lightly floured work surface for 5 minutes or until smooth. Alternatively, use an electric mixer with a dough hook. Place the dough in a greased bowl, cover and leave to rise in a warm place for 1 hour or until it has doubled in size.

3 Knead in the sultanas and shape the dough into 2 sausage shapes, each 25 cm/10 inches long. Carefully twist the 2 pieces together and pinch the ends to seal. Place the dough on the prepared baking tray, cover and leave in a warm place for a further 40 minutes.

4 Brush the loaf with the beaten egg and bake in a preheated oven, 220°C/425°F/Gas Mark 7, for 30 minutes or until golden-brown. Transfer the loaf to a wire rack and leave to cool. Dust with icing sugar before serving.

MAKES 1 LOAF

3 tbsp butter, cut into small pieces, plus extra for greasing
450 g/1 lb strong white bread flour, plus extra for dusting
1 tsp salt
1 sachet easy-blend dried yeast
1 tsp ground ginger
50 g/1¾ oz soft brown sugar
1 small mango, peeled, stoned and puréed
250 ml/9 fl oz hand-hot water
2 tbsp clear honey
125 g/4½ oz sultanas
1 egg, beaten
icing sugar, for dusting

NUTRITION
Calories *228*; Sugars *18 g*; Protein *6 g*; Carbohydrate *46 g*; Fat *4 g*; Saturates *2 g*

⭐⭐⭐ moderate

2 hrs 50 mins

30 mins

👨‍🍳 COOK'S TIP

You can tell when the bread is cooked as it will sound hollow when tapped on the base.

It is worth using a good quality olive oil for this cake as this will determine its flavour. The cake will keep well in an airtight tin.

Olive Oil, Fruit *and* Nut Cake

SERVES 8

1 tbsp butter for greasing
225 g/8 oz self-raising flour
50 g/1¾ oz caster sugar
125 ml/4 fl oz milk
4 tbsp orange juice
150 ml/5 fl oz olive oil
100 g/3½ oz mixed dried fruit
25 g/1 oz pine kernels

1 Grease an 18-cm/7-inch cake tin with butter and line with baking paper.

2 Sift the flour into a large bowl and stir in the caster sugar. Make a well in the centre of the dry ingredients and pour in the milk and orange juice. Stir the mixture with a wooden spoon, gradually beating in the flour and sugar.

3 Pour in the olive oil, stirring well so that all of the ingredients are thoroughly mixed. Stir the mixed dried fruit and pine kernels into the mixture and spoon into the prepared tin, spreading it out evenly. Smooth the surface with a palette knife.

4 Bake in a preheated oven, 180°C/350°F/Gas Mark 4, for about 45 minutes or until the cake is golden and firm to the touch.

5 Leave the cake to cool in the tin for a few minutes before transferring to a wire rack to cool completely. Serve the cake warm or cold and cut into slices.

NUTRITION

Calories *309*; Sugars *17 g*; Protein *4 g*; Carbohydrate *38 g*; Fat *17 g*; Saturates *3 g*

⭐⭐⭐   moderate
🟢   10 mins
🔵   45 mins

 COOK'S TIP

Pine kernels are best known as the flavouring ingredient in the classic Italian pesto, but here they give a delicate, slightly resinous flavour to this cake.

This cake is flavoured with clementine rind and juice, creating a very rich, buttery cake but one full of fresh fruit flavour.

Clementine Cake

1 Grease an 18-cm/7-inch round cake tin with butter and line the base with baking paper.

2 Pare the rind from the clementines and chop it finely. Cream the butter, sugar and clementine rind together in a bowl until pale and fluffy.

3 Gradually add the beaten eggs to the mixture, beating thoroughly after each addition.

4 Gently fold in the flour, ground almonds and cream. Spoon the mixture into the prepared tin.

5 Bake in a preheated oven, 180°C/350°F/Gas Mark 4, for 55–60 minutes or until a fine skewer inserted into the centre of the cake comes out clean. Remove from the oven and leave in the tin to cool slightly.

6 Meanwhile, make the glaze. Put the clementine juice into a small pan with the caster sugar. Bring to the boil over a low heat and simmer for 5 minutes.

7 Transfer the cake to a wire rack. Drizzle the glaze over the cake until it has been absorbed and sprinkle with the sugar cubes. Let cool, then serve in slices.

SERVES 8

175 g/6 oz butter, softened, plus extra
    for greasing
2 clementines
175 g/6 oz caster sugar
3 eggs, beaten
175 g/6 oz self-raising flour
3 tbsp ground almonds
3 tbsp single cream

glaze and topping
6 tbsp clementine juice
2 tbsp caster sugar
3 white sugar cubes, crushed

NUTRITION
Calories *427*; Sugars *32 g*; Protein *6 g*;
Carbohydrate *48 g*; Fat *25 g*; Saturates *13 g*

moderate

10 mins

1 hr 5 mins

 COOK'S TIP

If you prefer, chop the rind from the clementines in a food processor or blender together with the sugar at step 2. Tip the mixture into a bowl with the butter and begin to cream the mixture.

Polenta adds texture to this fruit cake, as well as a golden yellow colour. It also acts as a flour, binding the ingredients together.

Crunchy Fruit Cake

SERVES 8

100 g/3½ oz butter, softened, plus extra for greasing
100 g/3½ oz caster sugar
2 eggs, beaten
50 g/1¾ oz self-raising flour, sifted
1 tsp baking powder
100 g/3½ oz polenta
225 g/8 oz mixed dried fruit
25 g/1 oz pine kernels
grated rind of 1 lemon
4 tbsp lemon juice
2 tbsp milk

1 Grease an 18-cm/7-inch cake tin with a little butter and line the base with baking paper.

2 Cream the butter and sugar together in a bowl until light and fluffy.

3 Whisk in the beaten eggs, a little at a time, whisking thoroughly after each addition. Gently fold the flour, baking powder and polenta into the mixture until well blended.

4 Stir in the mixed dried fruit, pine kernels, grated lemon rind, lemon juice and milk. Spoon the mixture into the prepared tin and smooth the surface.

5 Bake in a preheated oven, 180°C/350°F/Gas Mark 4, for about 1 hour or until a fine skewer inserted into the centre of the cake comes out clean.

6 Remove from the oven and leave the cake to cool in the tin before turning out on to a wire rack to cool completely. Cut into slices and serve.

NUTRITION
Calories *328*; Sugars *33 g*; Protein *59 g*;
Carbohydrate *47 g*; Fat *15 g*; Saturates *7 g*

 moderate

5–10 mins

1 hr

 **COOK'S TIP**

To give a crumblier light fruit cake, omit the polenta and use 150 g/5½ oz self-raising flour instead.

This classic favourite is always popular with children and adults alike when it is served for afternoon tea.

Carrot Cake

1 Lightly grease a 20-cm/8-inch square cake tin with a little butter and line with baking paper.

2 Sift the flour, salt and ground cinnamon into a large bowl and stir in the brown sugar. Add the eggs and sunflower oil to the dry ingredients and mix well. Stir in the grated carrot, desiccated coconut and chopped walnuts.

3 Pour the mixture into the prepared tin and bake in a preheated oven, 180°C/350°F/Gas Mark 4, for 20–25 minutes or until just firm to the touch. Remove from the oven and leave the cake to cool in the tin.

4 Meanwhile, make the cheese frosting. Beat the butter, soft cheese, icing sugar and lemon juice together in a large bowl until fluffy and creamy.

5 Turn the cake out of the tin and cut into 12 bars or slices. Spread with the frosting and decorate with walnut pieces.

MAKES 12 BARS

1 tbsp butter for greasing
125 g/4½ oz self-raising flour
pinch of salt
1 tsp ground cinnamon
125 g/4½ oz soft brown sugar
2 eggs
100 ml/3½ fl oz sunflower oil
125 g/4½ oz carrots, peeled and finely grated
25 g/1 oz desiccated coconut
25 g/1 oz walnuts, chopped
walnut pieces, to decorate

frosting
4 tbsp butter, softened
50 g/1¾ oz full-fat soft cheese
225 g/8 oz icing sugar, sifted
1 tsp lemon juice

NUTRITION
Calories *294*; Sugars *32 g*; Protein *3 g*;
Carbohydrate *40 g*; Fat *15 g*; Saturates *5 g*

 moderate

5–10 mins

25 mins

 COOK'S TIP

For a moister cake, replace the coconut with 1 roughly mashed banana.

The lovely light and tangy flavour of the sponge is balanced by the lemony syrup poured over the top of the cake.

Lemon Syrup Cake

SERVES 8

1 tbsp butter for greasing
200 g/7 oz plain flour
2 tsp baking powder
200 g/7 oz caster sugar
4 eggs
150 ml/5 fl oz soured cream
grated rind 1 large lemon
4 tbsp lemon juice
150 ml/5 fl oz sunflower oil

syrup
4 tbsp icing sugar
3 tbsp lemon juice

1 Lightly grease a 20-cm/8-inch loose-bottomed round cake tin with the butter and line the base with baking paper.

2 Sift the flour and baking powder into a large bowl and stir in the caster sugar. Whisk the eggs, soured cream, lemon rind, lemon juice and oil together in a separate bowl.

3 Pour the egg mixture into the dry ingredients and mix thoroughly until evenly combined.

4 Pour the mixture into the prepared tin and bake in a preheated oven, 180°C/350°F/Gas Mark 4, for about 45–60 minutes or until well risen and golden-brown on top.

5 Meanwhile, make the syrup. Mix the icing sugar and lemon juice together in a small saucepan. Stir over a low heat until just beginning to bubble and turn syrupy.

6 As soon as the cake comes out of the oven prick the surface with a fine skewer, then brush the syrup over the top. Leave the cake to cool completely in the tin before turning out and serving.

COOK'S TIP

Pricking the surface of the hot cake with a skewer ensures that the syrup seeps right into the cake and the full flavour is absorbed.

NUTRITION
Calories *424*; Sugars *38 g*; Protein *6 g*;
Carbohydrate *58 g*; Fat *21 g*; Saturates *5 g*

 moderate

 1 hr 5 mins

 1 hr

Baking in a deep, fluted kugelhopf tin ensures that you create a cake with a stunning shape. The moist cake is full of fresh orange flavour.

Orange Kugelhopf Cake

1 Grease and flour a 25-cm/10-inch kugelhopf tin or deep ring mould.

2 Cream the butter and caster sugar together in a bowl until the mixture is light and fluffy. Add the egg yolks, one at a time, beating the mixture thoroughly after each addition.

3 Sift the flour, a pinch of salt and the baking powder into a separate bowl. Using a metal spoon, gently fold the dry ingredients and the orange juice alternately into the creamed mixture, working as lightly as possible. Stir in the orange flower water and orange rind.

4 Whisk the egg whites in a clean bowl until they form soft peaks, then fold them into the mixture in a figure-of-eight movement.

5 Pour the mixture into the prepared tin or ring mould and bake in a preheated oven, 180°C/350°F/Gas Mark 4, for about 50–55 minutes or until a fine skewer inserted into the centre of the cake comes out clean.

6 Put the orange juice and sugar in a small saucepan and bring to the boil over a low heat, then simmer for 5 minutes until the sugar has dissolved.

7 Remove the cake from the oven and leave to cool in the tin for 10 minutes. Prick the top of the cake with a fine skewer and brush over half of the syrup. Leave the cake to cool for a further 10 minutes. Invert the cake on to a wire rack placed over a deep plate and brush the syrup over the cake until it is covered. Serve warm or cold.

SERVES **6 – 8**

225 g/8 oz butter, softened, plus extra
   for greasing
425 g/15 oz plain flour, plus extra for dusting
225 g/8 oz caster sugar
4 eggs, separated
3 tsp baking powder
300 ml/10 fl oz fresh orange juice
1 tbsp orange flower water
1 tsp grated orange rind
salt

syrup
200 ml/7 fl oz orange juice
200 g/7 oz granulated sugar

NUTRITION
Calories *877*; Sugars *82 g*; Protein *12 g*;
Carbohydrate *137 g*; Fat *35 g*; Saturates *21 g*

★★★★ challenging

25 mins

55 mins

The addition of pieces of fresh apple and crunchy almonds to the cake mixture makes this beautifully moist yet with a crunch to it.

Spiced Apple Ring

SERVES 8

175 g/6 oz butter, softened, plus extra
   for greasing
175 g/6 oz caster sugar
3 eggs, beaten
175 g/6 oz self-raising flour
1 tsp ground cinnamon
1 tsp ground mixed spice
2 dessert apples, cored and grated
2 tbsp apple juice or milk
25 g/1 oz flaked almonds

1 Lightly grease a 25-cm/10-inch ovenproof ring mould with butter.

2 Cream the butter and sugar together in a large bowl until light and fluffy. Gradually add the beaten eggs, beating well after each addition.

3 Sift the flour and spices, then fold them into the creamed mixture.

4 Stir in the grated apples and the apple juice or milk and mix to a soft dropping consistency.

5 Sprinkle the flaked almonds round the base of the mould and spoon the cake mixture on top. Smooth the surface with the back of the spoon.

6 Bake the cake in a preheated oven, 180°C/350°F/Gas Mark 4, for 30 minutes or until well risen and a fine skewer inserted into the centre of the cake comes out clean.

7 Leave the cake to cool in the tin before turning out and transferring to a wire rack to cool completely. Serve the spiced apple ring cut into slices.

NUTRITION
Calories 379; Sugars 27 g; Protein 5 g; Carbohydrate 43 g; Fat 22 g; Saturates 13 g

⭐⭐⭐   moderate

     1 hr 5 mins

🕐   30 mins

👨‍🍳 COOK'S TIP

This cake can also be made in an 18-cm/7-inch round cake tin if you do not have an ovenproof ring mould.

This cake has a moist coffee and almond sponge on the base, covered with a deliciously crunchy spicy topping.

Coffee Streusel Cake

1 Grease a 23-cm/9-inch loose-bottomed round cake tin with butter and line with baking paper. Sift the flour and baking powder into a large bowl, then stir in the caster sugar.

2 Whisk the milk, eggs, butter and coffee mixture together in a separate bowl and pour on to the dry ingredients. Add the chopped almonds and mix lightly. Spoon the mixture into the prepared tin.

3 To make the topping, mix the flour and demerara sugar together in a large bowl. Add the butter and rub in with your fingertips until the mixture is crumbly. Sprinkle in the mixed spice and the water and bring the mixture together in loose crumbs. Sprinkle the topping evenly over the cake.

4 Bake in a preheated oven, 190°C/375°F/Gas Mark 5, for about 1 hour. Cover loosely with foil if the top begins to brown too quickly. Leave to cool in the tin, then turn out on to a wire rack to cool completely. Dust with icing sugar just before serving.

SERVES **8**

1 tbsp butter for greasing
275 g/9½ oz plain flour
1 tbsp baking powder
75 g/2¾ oz caster sugar
150 ml/5 fl oz milk
2 eggs
100 g/3½ oz butter, melted and cooled
2 tbsp instant coffee mixed with 1 tbsp boiling water
50 g/1¾ oz almonds, chopped
icing sugar, for dusting

topping

75 g/2¾ oz self-raising flour
75 g/2¾ oz demerara sugar
2 tbsp butter, cut into small pieces
1 tsp ground mixed spice
1 tbsp water

NUTRITION
Calories *409*; Sugars *21 g*; Protein *8 g*;
Carbohydrate *55 g*; Fat *19 g*; Saturates *10 g*

 moderate

10 mins

1 hr

This cake is full of flavour from the mixed fruits. The fruit gives the cake its sweetness so there is no need for extra sugar.

Sugar-free Fruit Cake

SERVES 8

125 g/4½ oz butter, cut into small pieces, plus extra for greasing
350 g/12 oz plain flour
2 tsp baking powder
1 tsp ground mixed spice
75 g/2¾ oz no-soak dried apricots, chopped
75 g/2¾ oz dried dates, chopped
75 g/2¾ oz glacé cherries, chopped
100 g/3½ oz raisins
125 ml/4 fl oz milk
2 eggs, beaten
grated rind of 1 orange
5–6 tbsp orange juice
3 tbsp clear honey

1 Grease a 20-cm/8-inch round cake tin with a little butter and line the base with baking paper.

2 Sift the flour, baking powder and ground mixed spice into a large bowl. Add the butter and rub it in with your fingertips until the mixture resembles fine breadcrumbs.

3 Carefully stir in the apricots, dates, glacé cherries and raisins with the milk, beaten eggs, grated orange rind and orange juice.

4 Stir in the honey and mix together to form a soft dropping consistency. Spoon into the prepared cake tin and smooth the surface.

5 Bake in a preheated oven, 180°C/350°F/Gas Mark 4, for 1 hour or until a fine skewer inserted into the centre of the cake comes out clean.

6 Leave the cake to cool in the tin before turning out.

NUTRITION
Calories 423; Sugars 34 g; Protein 8 g; Carbohydrate 68 g; Fat 16 g; Saturates 9 g

 moderate

1 hr 5 mins

1 hr

👨‍🍳 **COOK'S TIP**

For a fruity alternative, replace the honey with 1 mashed ripe banana.

This wonderfully spicy gingerbread is made even moister by the addition of chopped fresh apples.

Gingerbread

1 Grease a 23-cm/9-inch square cake tin with a little butter and line with baking paper.

2 Melt the butter, sugar and treacle in a saucepan over a low heat. Remove the pan from the heat and leave the mixture to cool.

3 Sift the flour, baking powder, bicarbonate of soda and ginger into a large bowl. Stir in the milk, beaten egg and cooled buttery liquid, followed by the chopped apples coated with the lemon juice.

4 Mix together gently, then pour the mixture into the prepared tin and smooth the surface.

5 Bake in a preheated oven, 160°C/325°F/Gas Mark 3, for 30–35 minutes or until the cake has risen and a fine skewer inserted into the centre of the cake comes out clean.

6 Leave the cake to cool in the tin before turning out and cutting into 12 bars.

MAKES 12 BARS

150 g/5½ oz butter, plus extra for greasing
175 g/6 oz soft brown sugar
2 tbsp black treacle
225 g/8 oz plain flour
1 tsp baking powder
2 tsp bicarbonate of soda
2 tsp ground ginger
150 ml/5 fl oz milk
1 egg, beaten
2 dessert apples, peeled, chopped and coated with 1 tbsp lemon juice

NUTRITION
Calories *248*; Sugars *21 g*; Protein *3 g*; Carbohydrate *36 g*; Fat *11 g*; Saturates *7 g*

 moderate

1 hr 15 mins

35 mins

COOK'S TIP

If you enjoy the flavour of ginger, try adding 25 g/1 oz finely chopped stem ginger to the mixture at Step 3.

These scones are light and buttery like traditional scones, but they have a deliciously rich flavour, which comes from the black treacle.

Treacle Scones

MAKES 8 SCONES

6 tbsp butter, cut into small pieces, plus extra for greasing
225 g/8 oz self-raising flour, plus extra for dusting
1 tbsp caster sugar
pinch of salt
1 dessert apple, peeled, cored and chopped
1 egg, beaten
2 tbsp black treacle
5 tbsp milk

1 Lightly grease a baking tray with a little butter.

2 Sift the flour, sugar and salt into a large bowl.

3 Add the butter and rub it in with your fingertips until the mixture resembles fine breadcrumbs.

4 Stir the chopped apple into the mixture until thoroughly combined.

5 Mix the egg, treacle and milk together in a jug. Add to the dry ingredients and mix well to form a soft dough.

6 Roll out the dough on a lightly floured work surface to a thickness of about 2 cm/¾ inch and cut out 8 scones, using a 5-cm/2-inch cutter.

7 Arrange the scones on the prepared baking tray and bake in a preheated oven, 220°C/425°F/Gas Mark 7, for 8–10 minutes.

8 Transfer the scones to a wire rack and leave to cool slightly. Serve split in half and spread with butter.

NUTRITION
Calories 208; Sugars 9 g; Protein 4 g;
Carbohydrate 30 g; Fat 9 g; Saturates 6 g

  moderate

15 mins

10 mins

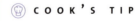 **COOK'S TIP**

These scones can be frozen, but are best thawed and eaten within 1 month.

These are an alternative to traditional scones, using sweet glacé cherries, which not only create colour but add a distinct flavour.

Cherry Scones

1 Lightly grease a baking tray with a little butter.

2 Sift the flour, sugar and salt into a large bowl. Add the butter and rub it in with your fingertips until the mixture resembles breadcrumbs.

3 Stir in the glacé cherries and sultanas, then add the beaten egg.

4 Reserve 1 tablespoon of the milk for glazing, then add the remainder to the mixture. Mix well to form a soft dough.

5 Roll out the dough on a lightly floured surface to a thickness of 2 cm/3/4 inch and cut out 8 scones, using a 5-cm/2-inch cutter.

6 Place the scones on the prepared baking tray and brush the tops with the reserved milk.

7 Bake in a preheated oven, 220°C/425°F/Gas Mark 7, for 8–10 minutes or until the scones are golden-brown.

8 Transfer the scones to a wire rack and leave to cool slightly. Serve split in half and spread with butter.

COOK'S TIP

These scones will freeze very successfully but they are best thawed and eaten within 1 month.

MAKES 8 SCONES

6 tbsp butter, cut into small pieces, plus extra for greasing
225 g/8 oz self-raising flour, plus extra for dusting
15 g/1/2 oz caster sugar
pinch of salt
40 g/1 1/2 oz glacé cherries, chopped
40 g/1 1/2 oz sultanas
1 egg, beaten
50 ml/2 fl oz milk

NUTRITION
Calories 211; Sugars 10 g; Protein 4 g; Carbohydrate 31 g; Fat 9 g; Saturates 6 g

 very easy
 10 mins
10 mins

These savoury muffins are an ideal accompaniment to soup, or they make a tasty alternative to sweet cakes for serving with tea or coffee.

Cranberry Muffins

MAKES 18 MUFFINS

1 tbsp butter for greasing
225 g/8 oz plain flour
2 tsp baking powder
½ tsp salt
50 g/1¾ oz caster sugar
4 tbsp butter, melted
2 eggs, beaten
200 ml/7 fl oz milk
100 g/3½ oz fresh cranberries
35 g/1¼ oz freshly grated Parmesan cheese

1 Lightly grease 2 bun tins with butter. Sift the flour, baking powder and salt into a large bowl. Stir in the caster sugar.

2 Mix the butter, beaten eggs and milk together in a separate bowl, then pour into the bowl of dry ingredients. Mix lightly until evenly combined. Finally, stir in the fresh cranberries.

3 Divide the mixture between the prepared tins. Sprinkle the grated Parmesan cheese over the top of each muffin.

4 Bake in a preheated oven, 200°C/400°F/Gas Mark 6, for about 20 minutes or until the muffins are well risen and golden-brown.

5 Leave the muffins to cool slightly in the tins, then transfer to a wire rack and leave to cool completely before serving.

NUTRITION
Calories 96; Sugars 4 g; Protein 3 g;
Carbohydrate 14 g; Fat 4 g; Saturates 2 g

 moderate

1 hr 5 mins

20 mins

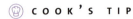 **COOK'S TIP**

For a sweet alternative to this recipe, replace the Parmesan cheese with demerara sugar at Step 3, if you prefer.

The sugar cubes give a lovely crunchy taste to this easy-to-make cake, which, served with cream, makes a splendid dessert.

Crispy-topped Fruit Bake

1 Grease a 900-g/2-lb loaf tin with butter and line with baking paper. Core, peel and finely dice the apples. Place them in a saucepan with the lemon juice, bring to the boil over a low heat, cover and simmer gently for about 10 minutes or until softened and pulpy. Beat thoroughly and leave to cool.

2 Sift the flour, baking powder and 1 teaspoon of cinnamon into a bowl, adding any bran remaining in the sieve. Stir in 115 g/4 oz blackberries and the muscovado sugar.

3 Make a well in the centre of the ingredients and add the egg, fromage frais and cooled apple purée. Mix well, then spoon the mixture into the prepared loaf tin. Smooth the surface.

4 Sprinkle with the remaining blackberries, pressing them down into the cake mixture, and top with the crushed sugar lumps. Bake in a preheated oven, 190°C/375°F/Gas Mark 5, for 40–45 minutes. Remove from the oven and leave to cool in the tin.

5 Remove the cake from the tin and peel away the lining paper. Serve dusted with cinnamon and decorated with extra blackberries and apple slices.

SERVES 10

1 tbsp butter for greasing
350 g/12 oz cooking apples
3 tbsp lemon juice
300 g/10½ oz wholemeal self-raising flour
½ tsp baking powder
1 tsp ground cinnamon, plus extra for dusting
175 g/6 oz prepared blackberries, thawed if frozen, plus extra to decorate
175 g/6 oz light muscovado sugar
1 egg, beaten
200 ml/7 fl oz low-fat natural fromage frais
55 g/2 oz white or brown sugar cubes, crushed lightly
sliced eating apple, to decorate

 COOK'S TIP

Try replacing the blackberries with blueberries. Use canned or frozen blueberries if the fresh fruit is unavailable.

NUTRITION

Calories 227; Sugars 30 g; Protein 5 g; Carbohydrate 53 g; Fat 1 g; Saturates 0.2 g

easy

15 mins

1 hr

Serve this moist, fruit-laden cake for a special occasion. It would also make an excellent Christmas or birthday cake.

Rich Fruit Cake

SERVES 8

1 tbsp butter, for greasing
175 g/6 oz stoned unsweetened dates
125 g/4½ oz no-soak dried prunes
200 ml/7 fl oz unsweetened orange juice
2 tbsp black treacle
1 tsp finely grated lemon rind
1 tsp finely grated orange rind
225 g/8 oz wholemeal self-raising flour
1 tsp mixed spice
125 g/4½ oz seedless raisins
125 g/4½ oz golden sultanas
125 g/4½ oz currants
125 g/4½ oz dried cranberries
3 large eggs, separated

to decorate

1 tbsp apricot jam, warmed
icing sugar, to dust
175 g/6 oz sugarpaste
strips of orange rind
strips of lemon rind

NUTRITION

Calories 772; Sugars 137 g; Protein 14 g;
Carbohydrate 179 g; Fat 5 g; Saturates 1 g

★★★   moderate

🟢   35 mins

🔵   1 hr 45 mins

1 Grease a deep 20-cm/8-inch round cake tin with butter and line with baking paper. Chop the dates and prunes and place in a saucepan. Pour over the orange juice and simmer over a low heat for 10 minutes. Remove the pan from the heat and beat the fruit mixture to a purée. Add the treacle and citrus rinds and leave to cool.

2 Sift the flour and spice into a large bowl, adding any bran remaining in the sieve. Add the dried fruits. When the date and prune mixture is cool, whisk in the egg yolks.

3 Whisk the egg whites in a clean bowl until stiff. Spoon the fruit mixture into the dry ingredients and mix together.

4 Using a metal spoon, gently fold in the egg whites. Transfer to the prepared tin and bake in a preheated oven, 160°C/325°F/Gas Mark 3, for 1½ hours. Remove from the oven and leave to cool in the tin.

5 Remove the cake from the tin and brush the top with jam. Dust the work surface with icing sugar and roll out the sugarpaste thinly. Lay the sugarpaste over the top of the cake and trim the edges. Decorate with strips of orange and lemon rind and serve.

This melt-in-the-mouth version of a favourite cake has a fraction of the fat of the traditional cake.

Carrot *and* Ginger Cake

1 Grease a 20-cm/8-inch round cake tin with the butter and line with baking paper.

2 Sift the flour, baking powder, bicarbonate of soda, ground ginger and salt into a large bowl. Stir in the sugar, carrots, stem ginger, fresh root ginger and raisins. Beat the eggs, sunflower oil and orange juice together, then pour into the bowl. Mix well.

3 Spoon the mixture into the prepared tin and bake in a preheated oven, 180°C/350°F/Gas Mark 4 for 1–1¼ hours or until firm to the touch and a fine skewer inserted into the centre of the cake comes out clean. Remove from the oven and leave to cool in the tin.

4 To make the frosting, place the soft cheese in a bowl and beat to soften. Sift the icing sugar into the cheese and add the vanilla essence. Mix well.

5 Remove the cooled cake from the tin and smooth the frosting over the top. Decorate the cake with grated carrot, chopped stem ginger and ground ginger, then serve.

 COOK'S TIP

If you prefer a nuttier cake, replace the raisins with pecan nuts or walnuts. Alternatively, add 25 g/1 oz raisins and 25 g/1 oz chopped walnuts at Step 2.

SERVES 10

1 tbsp butter, for greasing
225 g/8 oz plain flour
1 tsp baking powder
1 tsp bicarbonate of soda
2 tsp ground ginger
½ tsp salt
175 g/6 oz light muscovado sugar
225 g/8 oz carrots, grated
2 pieces chopped stem ginger
25 g/1 oz grated fresh root ginger
55 g/2 oz seedless raisins
2 medium eggs, beaten
3 tbsp sunflower oil
juice of 1 orange

frosting
225 g/8 oz low-fat soft cheese
4 tbsp icing sugar
1 tsp vanilla essence

to decorate
grated carrot
chopped finely stem ginger
ground ginger

NUTRITION
Calories *249*; Sugars *28 g*; Protein *7 g*; Carbohydrate *46 g*; Fat *6 g*; Saturates *1 g*

⭐⭐⭐   moderate

    15 mins

    1 hr 15 mins

Serve this moist, light sponge rolled up with an almond and strawberry fromage frais filling for a delicious tea-time treat.

Strawberry Roulade

SERVES 8

3 large eggs
125 g/4½ oz caster sugar
125 g/41/2 oz plain flour
1 tbsp hot water

filling
200 ml/7 fl oz low-fat fromage frais
1 tsp almond essence
225 g/8 oz small strawberries

to decorate
1 tbsp flaked almonds, toasted
1 tsp icing sugar

1 Line a 35 x 25-cm/14 x 10-inch Swiss roll tin with baking paper. Place the eggs in a heatproof bowl with the caster sugar. Place the bowl over a saucepan of hot, but not boiling water and whisk until pale and thick.

2 Remove the bowl from the pan. Sift in the flour and fold into the eggs with the hot water. Pour the mixture into the tin and bake in a preheated oven, 220°C/425°F/Gas Mark 7, for about 8–10 minutes or until golden and firm.

3 Invert the cake to a sheet of baking paper and remove the tin. Peel off the lining paper and roll up the sponge tightly along with the baking paper. Wrap in a tea towel and leave to cool.

4 Mix the fromage frais and almond essence together in a bowl. Reserving a few strawberries for decoration, wash, hull and slice the remainder. Leave the fromage frais mixture and the strawberries to chill in the refrigerator until required.

5 Unroll the sponge, spread the fromage frais mixture over the sponge and sprinkle with the sliced strawberries. Roll the sponge up again and transfer to a serving plate. Sprinkle with almonds and lightly dust with icing sugar. Decorate with the reserved strawberries.

NUTRITION
Calories *166*; Sugars *19 g*; Protein *6 g*;
Carbohydrate *30 g*; Fat *3 g*; Saturates *1 g*

✪✪✪✪ challenging

🖐 30 mins

🕐 10 mins

This cake is a great family favourite and is perfect served with afternoon tea on any occasion.

Coconut Cake

1 Grease a 900-g/2-lb loaf tin with a little butter and line the base with baking paper.

2 Sift the flour and a pinch of salt into a large bowl. Add the butter and rub in with your fingertips until the mixture resembles fine breadcrumbs.

3 Stir in the demerara sugar, desiccated coconut, eggs and milk and mix to a soft dropping consistency.

4 Spoon the mixture into the prepared tin and smooth the surface with a knife. Bake in a preheated oven, 160°C/325°F/Gas Mark 3, for 30 minutes.

5 Remove the cake from the oven and sprinkle with the extra coconut. Return the cake to the oven and cook for a further 30 minutes or until well risen and golden-brown, and a fine skewer inserted into the centre of the cake comes out clean.

6 Leave the cake to cool in the tin before turning out and transferring to a wire rack to cool completely before serving.

SERVES 6 – 8

100 g/3½ oz butter, cut into small pieces, plus extra for greasing
225 g/8 oz self-raising flour
100 g/3½ oz demerara sugar
100 g/3½ oz desiccated coconut, plus extra for sprinkling
2 eggs, beaten
4 tbsp milk
salt

NUTRITION
Calories *464*; Sugars *20 g*; Protein *8 g*; Carbohydrate *54 g*; Fat *26 g*; Saturates *18 g*

 very easy

 10 mins

🕐 30 mins

🍳 **COOK'S TIP**

The flavour of this cake is enhanced by storing it in a cool dry place for a few days before eating.

A mouth-watering dessert that is sure to impress your guests, especially if it is served with lots of whipped cream.

Almond Slices

SERVES 8

3 eggs
75 g/2¾ oz ground almonds
200 g/7 oz milk powder
200 g/7 oz sugar
½ tsp saffron strands
100 g/3½ oz unsalted butter
1 tbsp flaked almonds, to decorate

1 Beat the eggs together in a bowl and reserve.

2 Place the ground almonds, milk powder, sugar and saffron in a large bowl and stir to mix well.

3 Melt the butter in a small saucepan over a low heat. Pour the melted butter over the dry ingredients and mix well until thoroughly combined.

4 Add the reserved beaten eggs to the mixture and stir to blend well.

5 Spread the mixture in a shallow 15–20-cm/6–8-inch ovenproof dish and bake in a preheated oven, 160°C/325°F/Gas Mark 3, for 45 minutes. Test whether the cake is cooked through by piercing with the tip of a sharp knife or a skewer – it will come out clean if it is cooked thoroughly.

6 Cut the almond cake into slices. Decorate the almond slices with flaked almonds and transfer to serving plates. Serve hot or cold.

NUTRITION
Calories 416; Sugars 37 g; Protein 11 g;
Carbohydrate 38 g; Fat 26 g; Saturates 12 g

    easy

    5 mins

    45 mins

COOK'S TIP

These almond slices are best eaten hot, but they may also be served cold. They can be made a day or even a week in advance and reheated. They also freeze very well.

This variation of traditional Irish soda bread is best eaten on the day it has been baked, when it is deliciously fresh.

Soda Bread

1 Grease a baking tray with butter and dust lightly with flour.

2 Sift the flours, baking powder, bicarbonate of soda, sugar and salt into a large bowl and add any bran remaining in the sieve.

3 Beat the egg and yogurt together in a jug and pour the mixture into the dry ingredients. Mix together to form a soft and sticky dough.

4 Knead the dough on a lightly floured work surface for a few minutes until smooth, then shape the dough into a round about 5 cm/2 inches deep.

5 Transfer the dough to the prepared baking tray. Mark a cross shape in the centre of the top of the dough.

6 Bake in a preheated oven, 190°C/375°F/Gas Mark 5, for about 40 minutes or until the bread is golden-brown.

7 Transfer the loaf to a wire rack to cool completely. Cut into slices to serve.

MAKES 1 LOAF

1 tbsp butter, for greasing
300 g/10½ oz plain white flour, plus extra for dusting
300 g/10½ oz plain wholemeal flour
2 tsp baking powder
1 tsp bicarbonate of soda
25 g/1 oz caster sugar
1 tsp salt
1 egg, beaten
425 ml/15 fl oz natural yogurt

COOK'S TIP

For a fruity version of this soda bread, add 125 g/4½ oz raisins to the dry ingredients at step 2.

NUTRITION

Calories *203*; Sugars *7 g*; Protein *8 g*; Carbohydrate *42 g*; Fat *2 g*; Saturates *0 g*

 moderate

1 hr 10 mins

40 mins

Serve this spicy bread fresh from the oven with your favourite soup or a fresh tomato and onion salad for a light lunch or supper.

Spicy Bread

MAKES 1 LOAF

2 tbsp butter, cut into small pieces, plus extra for greasing
225 g/8 oz self-raising flour
100 g/3½ oz plain flour, plus extra for dusting
1 tsp baking powder
¼ tsp salt
¼ tsp cayenne pepper
2 tsp curry powder
2 tsp poppy seeds
150 ml/5 fl oz milk
1 egg, beaten

1 Lightly grease a baking tray with a little butter.

2 Sift both flours into a large bowl together with the baking powder, salt, cayenne, curry powder and poppy seeds.

3 Add the butter and rub it in with your fingertips until the mixture resembles breadcrumbs. Add the milk and the beaten egg and mix to a soft dough.

4 Knead the dough on to a lightly floured work surface for a few minutes. Shape the dough into a round and, using a knife, mark a cross in the centre of the top.

5 Bake in a preheated oven, 190°C/375°F/Gas Mark 5, for 45 minutes.

6 Transfer the bread to a wire rack and leave to cool. Serve in chunks or slices.

NUTRITION

Calories *122*; Sugars *1 g*; Protein *4 g*;
Carbohydrate *22 g*; Fat *3 g*; Saturates *2 g*

 moderate

 1 hr 10 mins

45 mins

🧑‍🍳 **COOK'S TIP**

If the bread looks as though it is browning too much, cover it with a piece of foil for the remainder of the cooking time.

This Mexican-style corn bread makes a great accompaniment to chilli or it can be eaten on its own as a tasty snack.

Chilli Corn Bread

1 Grease a 20-cm/8-inch square cake tin with butter and line the base with baking paper.

2 Sift the flour, polenta, baking powder and salt into a large bowl.

3 Add the green chilli and spring onions to the dry ingredients and mix well.

4 Beat the eggs together with the soured cream and sunflower oil in a jug, then pour the mixture into the bowl of dry ingredients. Mix together quickly and thoroughly. Pour the mixture into the prepared cake tin.

5 Bake in a preheated oven, 200°C/400°F/Gas Mark 6, for 20–25 minutes or until the loaf has risen and is lightly browned on top.

6 Leave the bread to cool slightly before turning out of the tin on to a wire rack to cool completely. Cut into bars or squares to serve.

MAKES 12 SQUARES

1 tbsp butter, for greasing
125 g/4½ oz plain flour
125 g/4½ oz polenta
1 tbsp baking powder
½ tsp salt
1 fresh green chilli, deseeded and finely chopped
5 spring onions, chopped finely
2 eggs
142 ml/4½ fl oz soured cream
125 ml/4 fl oz sunflower oil

NUTRITION
Calories *179*; Sugars *1 g*; Protein *3 g*; Carbohydrate *10 g*; Fat *14 g*; Saturates *3 g*

easy

5 mins

25 mins

🍳 **COOK'S TIP**

Add 125 g/4½ oz of sweetcorn kernels to the mixture at Step 3, if you prefer.

This is a quick bread to make. It is full of a wonderful cheese flavour and, to be enjoyed at its best, it should be eaten as fresh as possible.

Cheese *and* Chive Bread

SERVES 8

1 tbsp butter, for greasing
225 g/8 oz self-raising flour
1 tsp salt
1 tsp mustard powder
100 g/3½ oz mature cheese, grated
2 tbsp snipped fresh chives
1 egg, beaten
2 tbsp butter, melted
150 ml/5 fl oz milk

1 Grease a 23-cm/9-inch square cake tin with a little butter and line the base with baking paper.

2 Sift the flour, salt and mustard powder into a large bowl.

3 Reserve 3 tablespoons of the grated mature cheese for sprinkling over the top of the loaf before baking in the oven.

4 Stir the remaining grated cheese into the bowl, together with the chives. Mix together.

5 Add the beaten egg, melted butter and milk to the dry ingredients and stir the mixture thoroughly to combine.

6 Pour the mixture into the prepared tin, spreading it out evenly. Smooth the surface with a knife, then sprinkle over the reserved grated cheese.

7 Bake in a preheated oven, 190°C/375°F/Gas Mark 5, for about 30 minutes.

8 Remove the bread from the oven and leave to cool slightly in the tin, then turn out on to a wire rack to cool completely. Cut into triangles to serve.

NUTRITION
Calories *190*; Sugars *1 g*; Protein *7 g*; Carbohydrate *22 g*; Fat *9 g*; Saturates *5 g*

★★★   moderate
   25 mins
   30 mins

 COOK'S TIP

You can use any hard mature cheese of your choice for this recipe.

This bread is not at all like the shop-bought, ready-made garlic bread. Instead it has a subtle flavour and a soft texture.

Garlic Bread Rolls

1 Lightly grease a baking tray with a little butter.

2 Place the garlic and milk in a saucepan, bring to the boil over a low heat and simmer gently for 15 minutes. Remove the pan from the heat and leave to cool slightly, then process in a blender or food processor to purée the garlic.

3 Sift the flour and salt into a large bowl and stir in the dried yeast and mixed herbs.

4 Add the garlic-flavoured milk, sunflower oil and beaten egg to the dry ingredients and mix to form a dough.

5 Knead the dough on a lightly floured work surface for a few minutes until smooth and soft.

6 Place the dough in a lightly greased bowl, cover and leave to rise in a warm place for about 1 hour or until doubled in size.

7 Knock back the dough by kneading it for 2 minutes. Shape into 8 rolls and place on the prepared baking tray. Score the top of each roll with a knife, cover and leave for 15 minutes.

8 Brush the rolls with milk and sprinkle rock salt over the top.

9 Bake in a preheated oven, 220°C/425°F/Gas Mark 7, for 15–20 minutes. Transfer the rolls to a wire rack and leave to cool before serving.

MAKES 8 ROLLS

1 tbsp butter, for greasing
12 garlic cloves, peeled
350 ml/12 fl oz milk
450 g/1 lb strong white bread flour, plus extra for dusting
1 tsp salt
1 sachet easy-blend dried yeast
1 tbsp dried mixed herbs
2 tbsp sunflower oil
1 egg, beaten
milk, for brushing
rock salt, for sprinkling

NUTRITION
Calories 265; Sugars 3 g; Protein 10 g; Carbohydrate 46 g; Fat 6 g; Saturates 2 g

 easy

1 hr 45 mins

35 mins

This is a delicious Italian bread made with olive oil. The topping of red onions and thyme is particularly flavoursome.

Mini Focaccia

SERVES 4

2 tbsp olive oil, plus extra for brushing
350 g/12 oz strong white flour, plus extra for dusting
½ tsp salt
1 sachet easy-blend dried yeast
250 ml/9 fl oz hand-hot water
100 g/3½ oz stoned green or black olives, halved

topping
2 red onions, sliced
2 tbsp olive oil
1 tsp sea salt
1 tbsp fresh thyme leaves

1 Lightly brush several baking trays with olive oil. Sift the flour and salt into a large bowl, then stir in the yeast. Pour in the olive oil and water and mix together to form a dough.

2 Knead the dough on a lightly floured work surface for about 5 minutes. Alternatively, use an electric mixer with a dough hook.

3 Place the dough in a greased bowl, cover and leave to rise in a warm place for about 1–1½ hours or until the dough has doubled in size. Knock back the dough by kneading it again for 1–2 minutes.

4 Knead half of the olives into the dough. Divide the dough into quarters and shape the quarters into rounds. Place them on the prepared baking trays and push your fingers into the dough to create a dimpled effect.

5 To make the topping, sprinkle the red onions and remaining olives over the rounds. Drizzle the olive oil over the top and sprinkle with the sea salt and thyme leaves. Cover and leave to rise for 30 minutes.

6 Bake in a preheated oven, 190°C/375°F/Gas Mark 5, for 20–25 minutes or until the focaccia are golden.

7 Transfer to a wire rack and leave to cool before serving.

NUTRITION
Calories *439*; Sugars *3 g*; Protein *9 g*; Carbohydrate *71 g*; Fat *15 g*; Saturates *2 g*

easy

2 hrs 15 mins

25 mins

These white rolls have the addition of finely chopped sun-dried tomatoes. The tomatoes are sold in jars and are available at most supermarkets.

Sun-dried Tomato Rolls

1 Lightly grease a large baking tray with a little butter.

2 Sift the flour and salt into a large bowl. Stir in the yeast, then pour in the butter, milk and eggs. Mix to form a dough.

3 Knead the dough on a lightly floured work surface for about 5 minutes. Alternatively, use an electric mixer with a dough hook.

4 Place the dough in a greased bowl, cover and leave to rise in a warm place for 1–1½ hours or until the dough has doubled in size. Knock back the dough for 2–3 minutes.

5 Knead the sun-dried tomatoes into the dough, sprinkling the work surface with a little extra flour as the tomatoes are quite oily.

6 Divide the dough into 8 equal-sized balls and place them on the prepared baking tray. Cover and leave to rise for about 30 minutes or until the rolls have doubled in size.

7 Brush the rolls with milk and bake in a preheated oven, 230°C/450°F/Gas Mark 8, for 10–15 minutes or until the rolls are golden-brown.

8 Transfer the rolls to a wire rack and leave to cool slightly before serving.

 COOK'S TIP

Add some finely chopped anchovies or olives to the dough at Step 5 for extra flavour, if liked.

MAKES 8 ROLLS

1 tbsp butter, for greasing
225 g/8 oz strong white bread flour, plus extra for dusting
½ tsp salt
1 sachet easy-blend dried yeast
100 g/3½ oz butter, melted and cooled slightly
3 tbsp milk, warmed
2 eggs, beaten
50 g/1¾ oz sun-dried tomatoes, well drained and finely chopped
milk, for brushing

NUTRITION
Calories 214; Sugars 1 g; Protein 5 g; Carbohydrate 22 g; Fat 12 g; Saturates 7 g

easy

2 hrs 15 mins

15 mins

These home-made scones are given an interesting flavour by adding grated mature cheese and mustard to the mixture.

Cheese *and* Mustard Scones

MAKES 8 SCONES

4 tbsp butter, cut into small pieces, plus extra for greasing
225 g/8 oz self-raising flour, plus extra for dusting
1 tsp baking powder
pinch of salt
125 g/4½ oz mature cheese, grated
1 tsp mustard powder
150 ml/5 fl oz milk
pepper

1 Lightly grease a baking tray with a little butter.

2 Sift the flour, baking powder and salt into a large bowl. Add the butter and rub it in with your fingertips until the mixture resembles breadcrumbs.

3 Stir in the cheese, mustard powder and enough milk to form a soft dough.

4 Knead the dough very lightly on a lightly floured work surface, then flatten it out with the palm of your hand to a depth of about 2.5 cm/1 inch.

5 Cut the dough into 8 wedges with a knife. Brush each one with a little milk and sprinkle with pepper to taste.

6 Bake in a preheated oven, 220°C/425°F/Gas Mark 7, for 10–15 minutes or until the scones are golden-brown.

7 Transfer the scones to a wire rack and leave to cool slightly before serving.

NUTRITION
Calories *218*; Sugars *1 g*; Protein *7 g*; Carbohydrate *22 g*; Fat *12 g*; Saturates *7 g*

 very easy

 15 mins

 15 mins

 **COOK'S TIP**

Scones should be eaten on the day they are made as they quickly go stale. Serve them split in half and spread with butter.

This flavoursome bread contains only the minimum amount of fat. Serve with a bowl of hot soup for a filling and nutritious light meal.

Savoury Pepper Bread

1 Grease a 23-cm/9-inch round springform cake tin with butter. Place the peppers on a grill rack and cook under a preheated hot grill until the skin is charred. Cool for 10 minutes, peel off the skin and chop the flesh. Slice the tomatoes into strips, place in a bowl and pour over the water. Leave to soak.

2 Place the yeast and sugar in a jug, pour over the hand-hot water and leave for 10–15 minutes until frothy. Sift the flour into a bowl and add 1 teaspoon of dried rosemary. Make a well in the centre and pour in the yeast mixture.

3 Add the tomato purée, tomatoes and soaking liquid, peppers, fromage frais and half the salt. Mix to form a soft dough. Knead the dough on a lightly floured work surface for 3–4 minutes until smooth. Place in a lightly floured bowl, cover and leave in a warm place for 40 minutes until doubled in size.

4 Knead the dough again and place in the prepared tin. Using a wooden spoon, form 'dimples' in the surface. Cover and leave for 30 minutes. Brush with olive oil and sprinkle with rosemary and salt. Bake in a preheated oven, 220°C/425°F/Gas Mark 7, for 35–40 minutes. Remove from the oven and cool in the tin for 10 minutes, then release from the tin and leave to cool on a wire rack before serving.

COOK'S TIP

For a quick, filling snack serve the bread with a bowl of hot soup in winter, or a crisp leaf salad in summer.

SERVES 8

1 tbsp butter, for greasing
1 small red pepper, halved and deseeded
1 small green pepper, halved and deseeded
1 small yellow pepper, halved and deseeded
55 g/2 oz dry packet sun-dried tomatoes
50 ml/2 fl oz boiling water
2 tsp dried yeast
1 tsp caster sugar
150 ml/5 fl oz hand-hot water
450 g/1 lb strong white bread flour, plus extra for dusting
2 tsp dried rosemary
2 tbsp tomato purée
150 ml/5 fl oz low-fat natural fromage frais
1 tbsp coarse salt
1 tbsp olive oil

NUTRITION
Calories 468; Sugars 11 g; Protein 16 g; Carbohydrate 97 g; Fat 5 g; Saturates 1 g

challenging

2 hrs

50 mins

Biscuits

Nothing can compare with a home-made biscuit for bringing a touch of pleasure to a coffee break or tea-time. This selection of delicious biscuits and after-dinner treats will tantalize your taste buds and keep you coming back for more. Moreish biscuits like Citrus Crescents, Meringues, Rock Drops and Gingernuts are quick, easy and satisfying to make. You can easily vary any of the ingredients listed to suit your taste – the possibilities for inventiveness when making biscuits are endless and this chapter shows you how.

These savoury biscuits have a delicious buttery flavour. Make sure you use a mature cheese for the best flavour.

Cheese Sablés

MAKES 35 BISCUITS

150 g/5½ oz butter, cut into small pieces, plus extra for greasing
150 g/5½ oz plain flour, plus extra for dusting
150 g/5½ oz mature cheese, grated
1 egg yolk
sesame seeds, for sprinkling

1 Lightly grease several baking trays with a little butter.

2 Mix the flour and cheese together in a large bowl.

3 Add the butter to the cheese and flour mixture and mix with your fingertips until combined.

4 Stir in the egg yolk and mix to form a dough. Wrap the dough in clingfilm and leave to chill in the refrigerator for about 30 minutes.

5 Roll out the cheese dough thinly on a lightly floured work surface. Cut out 6-cm/2½-inch rounds, re-rolling the trimmings to make about 35 rounds.

6 Place the rounds on to the prepared baking trays and sprinkle the sesame seeds over the top of them.

7 Bake in a preheated oven, 200°C/400°F/Gas Mark 6, for 20 minutes until the sablés are lightly golden.

8 Carefully transfer the cheese sablés to a wire rack and leave to cool slightly before serving.

NUTRITION
Calories 67; Sugars 0 g; Protein 2 g; Carbohydrate 3 g; Fat 5 g; Saturates 3 g

easy

50 mins

20 mins

COOK'S TIP

Cut out any shape you like for your savoury biscuits. Children will enjoy them cut into animal or other fun shapes.

These spicy biscuits are perfect to serve with fruit salad or ice cream for an easy instant dessert.

Spiced Biscuits

1 Lightly grease 2 baking trays with a little butter.

2 Cream the butter and sugar together in a large bowl and beat until light and fluffy.

3 Sift the flour, a pinch of salt, the bicarbonate of soda, cinnamon, coriander, nutmeg and cloves into the creamed mixture.

4 Stir the dark rum into the creamed mixture.

5 Using 2 teaspoons, place small mounds of the mixture on to the baking trays, placing them 7.5 cm/3 inches apart to allow for spreading during cooking. Flatten each one slightly with the back of a spoon.

6 Bake in a preheated oven, 180°C/350°F/Gas Mark 4, for 10–12 minutes or until golden-brown.

7 Transfer the biscuits to wire racks to cool and crispen before serving.

MAKES 12 BISCUITS

175 g/6 oz unsalted butter, plus extra for greasing
175 g/6 oz dark muscovado sugar
225 g/8 oz plain flour
½ tsp bicarbonate of soda
1 tsp ground cinnamon
½ tsp ground coriander
½ tsp ground nutmeg
¼ tsp ground cloves
2 tbsp dark rum
salt

NUTRITION
Calories 117; Sugars 8 g; Protein 1 g;
Carbohydrate 15 g; Fat 6 g; Saturates 4 g

moderate
35 mins
12 mins

 COOK'S TIP

Use the back of a fork to flatten the biscuits slightly before baking.

These are moist cake-like squares with a lovely spicy flavour. They smell simply wonderful while cooking.

Cinnamon *and* Seed Squares

MAKES 12 SQUARES

250 g/9 oz butter, softened, plus extra for greasing
250 g/9 oz caster sugar
3 eggs, beaten
250 g/9 oz self-raising flour
½ tsp bicarbonate of soda
1 tbsp ground cinnamon
150 ml/5 fl oz soured cream
100 g/3½ oz sunflower seeds

1 Grease a 23-cm/9-inch square cake tin with butter and line the base with baking paper.

2 Cream the butter and caster sugar together in a large bowl until light and fluffy. Gradually add the beaten eggs to the mixture, beating thoroughly after each addition.

3 Sift the flour, bicarbonate of soda and cinnamon into the creamed mixture and fold in gently, using a metal spoon. Spoon in the soured cream and sunflower seeds and gently mix until well combined.

4 Spoon the mixture into the prepared cake tin and smooth the surface with the back of a spoon or a knife.

5 Bake in a preheated oven, 180°C/350°F/Gas Mark 4, for about 45 minutes or until the mixture is firm to the touch when pressed with a finger.

6 Loosen the edges with a round-bladed knife, then turn out on to a wire rack to cool completely. Slice into 12 squares before serving.

NUTRITION
Calories 397; Sugars 23 g; Protein 6 g;
Carbohydrate 40 g; Fat 25 g; Saturates 14 g

easy

1 hr 10 mins

45 mins

COOK'S TIP
These moist squares will freeze well and will keep for up to 1 month.

Nothing compares to the taste of these freshly baked authentic gingernuts, which have a lovely hint of orange.

Gingernuts

1 Lightly grease several baking trays with a little butter.

2 Sift the flour, salt, sugar, ginger and bicarbonate of soda into a large bowl.

3 Heat the butter and golden syrup together in a saucepan over a very low heat until the butter has melted.

4 Remove the pan from the heat and leave the butter and syrup mixture to cool slightly, then pour it on to the dry ingredients.

5 Add the egg and orange rind and mix thoroughly to form a dough.

6 Using your hands, carefully shape the dough into 30 even-sized balls.

7 Place the balls well apart on the prepared baking trays, then flatten them slightly with your fingers.

8 Bake in a preheated oven, 160°C/325°F/Gas Mark 3, for 15–20 minutes, then carefully transfer the biscuits to a wire rack to cool before serving.

MAKES 30 BISCUITS

125 g/4½ oz butter, plus extra for greasing
350 g/12 oz self-raising flour
pinch of salt
200 g/7 oz caster sugar
1 tbsp ground ginger
1 tsp bicarbonate of soda
75 g/2¾ oz golden syrup
1 egg, beaten
1 tsp grated orange rind

NUTRITION
Calories *106*; Sugars *9 g*; Protein *1 g*;
Carbohydrate *18 g*; Fat *4 g*; Saturates *2 g*

  moderate

10 mins

20 mins

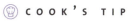 **COOK'S TIP**

Store these biscuits in an airtight container and eat them within 1 week.

These crunchy biscuits will be popular with children of all ages as they contain a firm favourite – peanut butter.

Peanut Butter Cookies

MAKES 20 BISCUITS

125 g/4½ oz butter, softened, plus extra for greasing
150 g/5½ oz chunky peanut butter
225 g/8 oz granulated sugar
1 egg, beaten lightly
150 g/5½ oz plain flour
½ tsp baking powder
pinch of salt
75 g/2¾ oz natural unsalted peanuts, chopped

1 Lightly grease 2 baking trays with a little butter.

2 Beat the butter and peanut butter together in a large bowl.

3 Gradually add the sugar and beat well.

4 Add the beaten egg, a little at a time, beating well after each addition until it is thoroughly combined.

5 Sift the flour, baking powder and salt into the peanut butter mixture.

6 Add the chopped peanuts and mix to form a soft dough. Wrap the dough in clingfilm and leave to chill in the refrigerator for about 30 minutes.

7 Shape the dough into 20 balls and place them on the prepared baking trays about 5 cm/2 inches apart to allow for spreading during cooking. Flatten them slightly with your hand.

8 Bake in a preheated oven, 190°C/375°F/Gas Mark 5, for 15 minutes or until golden-brown. Transfer the biscuits to a wire rack and leave to cool.

NUTRITION
Calories *186*; Sugars *13 g*; Protein *4 g*;
Carbohydrate *19 g*; Fat *11 g*; Saturates *5 g*

 easy

 40 mins

🕐 15 mins

👑 **COOK'S TIP**

For a crunchy bite and sparkling appearance, sprinkle the biscuits with demerara sugar before baking.

These oaty, fruity biscuits couldn't be easier to make and are delicious with a well-earned cup of tea!

Oat *and* Raisin Biscuits

1 Lightly grease 2 baking trays with a little butter.

2 Cream the butter and sugar together in a large bowl until light and fluffy.

3 Gradually add the beaten egg, beating well after each addition, until thoroughly combined.

4 Sift the flour, salt and baking powder into the creamed mixture. Mix gently. Add the porridge oats, raisins and sesame seeds and mix thoroughly.

5 Place spoonfuls of the mixture spaced well apart on the prepared baking trays to allow for expansion during cooking. Flatten them slightly with the back of a spoon.

6 Bake the biscuits in a preheated oven, 180°C/350°F/Gas Mark 4, for about 15 minutes.

7 Remove the biscuits from the oven and leave to cool for a few minutes on the baking trays. Carefully transfer the biscuits to a wire rack and leave to cool completely before serving.

MAKES 10 BISCUITS

4 tbsp butter, plus extra for greasing
125 g/4½ oz caster sugar
1 egg, beaten
50 g/1¾ plain flour
½ tsp salt
½ tsp baking powder
175 g/6 oz porridge oats
125 g/4½ oz raisins
2 tbsp sesame seeds

COOK'S TIP

To enjoy these biscuits at their best, store them in an airtight container.

NUTRITION

Calories *227*; Sugars *22 g*; Protein *4 g*;
Carbohydrate *39 g*; Fat *7 g*; Saturates *3 g*

easy

50 mins

15 mins

For a sweet treat, try these attractive crescent-shaped biscuits, which have a lovely citrus tang to them.

Citrus Crescents

MAKES 25 BISCUITS

100 g/3½ oz butter, softened, plus extra for greasing
75 g/2¾ oz caster sugar, plus extra for dusting (optional)
1 egg, separated
200 g/7 oz plain flour, plus extra for dusting
grated rind of 1 orange
grated rind of 1 lemon
grated rind of 1 lime
2–3 tbsp orange juice

1 Lightly grease 2 baking trays with a little butter.

2 Cream the butter and sugar together in a large bowl until light and fluffy, then gradually beat in the egg yolk.

3 Sift the flour into the creamed mixture and mix until blended. Add the citrus rinds with enough of the orange juice to make a soft dough.

4 Roll out the dough on a lightly floured work surface. Stamp out rounds using a 7.5-cm/3-inch biscuit cutter. Make crescent shapes by cutting away a quarter of each round. Re-roll the trimmings to make about 25 crescents.

5 Place the crescents on the prepared baking trays, spacing them apart to allow room for expansion during cooking. Prick the surface of each crescent with a fork.

6 Lightly whisk the egg white in a small bowl and brush it over the biscuits. Dust with extra caster sugar, if using.

7 Bake in a preheated oven, 200°C/400°F/Gas Mark 6, for 12–15 minutes. Carefully transfer the biscuits to a wire rack and leave to cool and crispen before serving.

COOK'S TIP

Store the citrus crescents in an airtight container. Alternatively, they can be frozen for up to 1 month.

NUTRITION

Calories 72; Sugars 3 g; Protein 1 g; Carbohydrate 10 g; Fat 4 g; Saturates 2 g

moderate

10 mins

15 mins

These elegant biscuits are perfect for afternoon tea or they can be served with vanilla ice cream for a delicious dessert.

Shortbread Fantails

1 Lightly grease a 20-cm/8-inch shallow round cake tin with butter.

2 Cream the butter, the granulated sugar and the icing sugar together in a large bowl until light and fluffy.

3 Sift the flour and a pinch of salt into the creamed mixture. Add the orange flower water and mix to form a soft dough.

4 Roll out the dough on a lightly floured work surface to a 20-cm/8-inch round and place in the prepared tin. Prick the dough well and score into 8 triangles with a round-bladed knife.

5 Bake in a preheated oven, 150°C/300°F/Gas Mark 2, for 30-35 minutes or until the shortbread is crisp and a pale golden colour.

6 Remove from the oven and sprinkle the shortbread with caster sugar, then cut along the marked lines to make the 8 fantails.

7 Leave the shortbread to cool in the tin. Store in an airtight container.

SERVES 8

125 g/4½ oz butter, softened, plus extra for greasing
40 g/1½ oz granulated sugar
25 g/1 oz icing sugar
225 g/8 oz plain flour, plus extra for dusting
2 tsp orange flower water
caster sugar, for sprinkling
salt

NUTRITION
Calories *248*; Sugars *10 g*; Protein *3 g*; Carbohydrate *32 g*; Fat *13 g*; Saturates *9 g*

easy

40 mins

35 mins

🍳 COOK'S TIP

For a crunchy addition, sprinkle 2 tablespoons of chopped mixed nuts over the top of the fantails before baking.

These rock drops are more substantial than a crisp biscuit. Serve them fresh from the oven to enjoy them at their best.

Rock Drops

MAKES 8 BISCUITS

100 g/3½ oz butter, cut into small pieces, plus extra for greasing
200 g/7 oz plain flour
2 tsp baking powder
75 g/2¾ oz demerara sugar
100 g/3½ oz sultanas
25 g/1 oz glacé cherries, chopped finely
1 egg, beaten
2 tbsp milk

1 Lightly grease a baking tray with a little butter.

2 Sift the flour and baking powder into a large bowl. Add the butter and rub it in with your fingertips until the mixture resembles breadcrumbs.

3 Stir in the sugar, sultanas and chopped glacé cherries.

4 Add the beaten egg and milk to the mixture and mix to form a soft dough.

5 Spoon 8 mounds of the mixture on to the prepared baking tray, spacing them well apart to allow for expansion during cooking.

6 Bake in a preheated oven, 200°C/400°F/Gas Mark 6, for 15–20 minutes or until firm to the touch when pressed with a finger.

7 Remove the rock drops from the baking tray. Either serve piping hot from the oven or transfer to a wire rack and leave to cool before serving.

NUTRITION
Calories *270*; Sugars *21 g*; Protein *4 g*; Carbohydrate *41 g*; Fat *11 g*; Saturates *7 g*

easy

5–10 mins

20 mins

 COOK'S TIP

For convenience, prepare the dry ingredients in advance and just before cooking stir in the liquid.

These are just as meringues should be – as light as air and at the same time crisp and melt-in-the-mouth.

Meringues

1 Line 3 baking trays with sheets of baking paper.

2 Using an electric hand-held whisk or a balloon whisk, whisk the egg whites and a pinch of salt together in a large, clean bowl until stiff. (You should be able to turn the bowl upside down without any movement from the whisked egg whites.)

3 Whisk in the granulated sugar, a little at a time – the meringue should begin to look glossy at this stage.

4 Sprinkle in the caster sugar, a little at a time and whisk until all the sugar has been incorporated and the meringue is thick, white and forms peaks.

5 Transfer the meringue mixture to a piping bag fitted with a 2-cm/^{3}/$_4$-inch star nozzle. Pipe about 26 small whirls on to the prepared baking trays.

6 Bake in a preheated oven, 120°C/250°F/Gas Mark ^{1}/$_2$, for 1^1/$_2$ hours or until the meringues are pale golden in colour and can be easily lifted off the paper. Leave them to cool in the turned-off oven overnight.

7 Just before serving, sandwich the meringues together in pairs with the cream and arrange on a serving plate.

 COOK'S TIP

For a finer texture, replace the granulated sugar with caster sugar.

MAKES 13 MERINGUES

4 egg whites
125 g/4^1/$_2$ oz granulated sugar
125 g/4^1/$_2$ oz caster sugar
salt
300 ml/10 fl oz double cream, whipped lightly, to serve

NUTRITION

Calories *183*; Sugars *21 g*; Protein *1 g*; Carbohydrate *21 g*; Fat *11 g*; Saturates *7 g*

easy

15 mins

1 hr 30 mins

Index